ABBEYS AND PRIORIES

OF

WALES

R.N. Cooper

CHRISTOPHER DAVIES

Published by Christopher Davies (Publishers) Limited,
P.O. Box 403, Sketty, Swansea, SA2 9BE.

ISBN 0 7154 07120

Typeset in ITC Bookman by Words, Swansea.
Printed and bound in Wales by Dinefwr Press, Llandybie, Dyfed.
Cover design by Northcott Studios, Swansea.

Dedicated to the Memory of
Reverend Cyril Rees
Bethel, Penclawdd

CONTENTS

Farther along the road,
And not wholly cut off from a world of richer fields,
There is the ruin of an abbey ...
It is but a cave of masonry
Topped by umbrageous ivy that swells
Over its edge like froth over a tankard.
Altar and bells and books
And large abbatic oven are gone.
Only the jackdaw remains.

Edward Thomas. *Wales.* (Extract from Chapter 5)

Introduction

Wales has long been famed for its castles - buildings and ruins that strike a dramatic posture dominating hilltops, estuaries and riversides. The castles are seen by visitors as symbols of much that is typical of Welsh history and landscape. And yet these structures were essentially devices of war, the missile bases of their age. In their own time they could hardly have been regarded as anything but an eyesore, an abomination on the landscape, a symbol of the intruder's power. Had local authority planning permission been required in the medieval period then the castles would certainly have been refused it on aesthetic grounds alone. And who would have permitted buildings that so grossly distorted the development of the period's principal towns? Today these same places are regarded as major tourist attractions and assets to the landscape.

On the other hand those other ruins of Wales, the abbeys and priories of the Middle Ages, have less renown. It is ironic that such buildings, which were built with aesthetic considerations very much in mind, are now, with a few notable exceptions, crumbling and forgotten. They were not built to dominate the landscape, indeed, many were built in such a way as to escape the attention of unwelcome eyes. As survivals of their age they represent the highest expressions of the cultures, both Welsh and English, that fed the minds of their builders. Sometimes they were inextricably linked with the conquest and may be viewed as just another facet of the invasion. Even in this instance the abbey or priory represented something rather finer than the mere bludgeoning of a people into submission.

One of the main premises of this book is that the remains of the abbeys and priories of Wales have not been given credit for all that they have to offer the visitor. In these sites there is much to be seen that is beautiful and much that is highly significant in the history of Wales. They tell more of the hopes and fears of the people before and after they lost their independence than do many of the castles. Frequently they occupy sites of great natural beauty and positively enhance the landscape. Often the bald shape of a castle's curtain wall should be recognised for what it is, an ugly ruin. The same is rarely, if ever, true of the ecclesiastical ruins with which this work is concerned. It is to be hoped that the continuous decline of some sites will be halted before the ruins are totally lost. In the meantime a more modest hope is that this account of the remains of the abbeys and priories of Wales will give some idea of what is to be seen today. Coupled with a short history of each house and a brief interpretation of the ruins and structures still to be seen it may even encourage a livelier and wider interest in the sites.

Part I

A BRIEF HISTORY

SITES OF ABBEYS AND PRIORIES IN WALES

Key:
1. Bassaleg
2. Malpas
3. Llantarnam
4. Grace Dieu
5. Monmouth
6. Tintern
7. St Kynemark
8. Chepstow

12

The Celtic background

In the early period of Christianity the monastic ideal found very considerable popularity in Wales. Primitive monastic communities were established in various places and these became noted for their ascetic way of life. Many of these communities were located on remote islands where the monastic traditions were maintained on the basis of escaping from the secular life. This strain of separateness from secular life coupled with a tendency to asceticism characterised the early Welsh monasteries and was associated with later survivals in the Norman period. It was the Cistercians who found most success in Wales in the medieval period and to a large extent this must have been because of their simple way of life in the remote corners of the country, an echo of the Welsh idea of monastic life. Another strain in the Cistercian ideal was the importance of physical labour, especially on the land. This too was an important element in the early Celtic houses where a tri-partite division of the community was sought. One group of unskilled members of the community would be set to labour on the land, another group to labour within the monastery. Those fitted for maintaining the worship of the church were mainly confined to the monastery for that purpose although some would be engaged in the missionary work that was an important aspect of most communities. These communities, in their remote settings and with the most primitive buildings, have left no survivals except a few carved stones and crosses. But in the Welsh mind those early ideals survived and even in the Norman period the hermit's life was respected and commonly sought after.

By the time of the Norman invasion the monastic communities were greatly changed. There was a degree of informality and casual organisation about the Welsh monasteries that must have infuriated the Normans to whom a monastery was either an abbey or priory, belonging to an established order with rules of conduct and a hierarchy of authority. In Wales the celibacy of the monks was no longer the norm. In many communities the monks were in fact clerics and served churches through a wide area. A looser organisational structure led to the 'clas' developing, a community of monks functioning round a scriptorium and a scholastic body. Within the 'clas' a bishop might have a seat and the area of influence of the 'clas' was commensurate with the bishop's authority. Thus the church in Wales developed in close alliance with the monastic communities providing a sense of slow but steady evolution. The lack of powerful hierarchical structures controlling the church may have allowed for ever new models of organisation to develop and meet the religious needs of the nation. If Wales had remained independent it would be interesting to speculate how the church would be organised today.

But all was not well with the Welsh monastic life. During the period of the Norse raids the monasteries had suffered the most severe deprivations. Many houses were near the coast or on islands and were plundered with some regularity. It may be that some communities armed themselves against this threat and thus developed a new and less endearing tradition for their monks. With their lack of close organisation or powerful authority the monasteries were not really meeting these exigencies and appear to have been in an unhealthy state by the time of the Normans. Gerald of Wales, although not a partial observer, was generally caustic and disapproving about those survivals of the Welsh monasteries that he came across. Welsh monastic life was in no fit condition to combat the influence of the Normans with their well organised monastic orders accompanying the invading forces.

The Norman conquest

The Norman conquest of Wales was nothing like that of England. William I, the Conqueror, proscribed military adventures in Wales. The Marcher Lords may have chaffed at the bit but they did not make serious inroads into the Celtic lands. William was quite happpy that his status as overlord of Wales was adequate to his needs and those of his kingdom - for the present. On his death, however, frustrated noblemen were released from these shackles to take such lands as they could gain. So the conquest of Wales was, from the start, an affair of private military adventurism rather than the organised attack on one nation by another. The attacks took place as opportunity offered and this was amply provided by the disunity of the Welsh themselves as well as by the willingness of the Norman kings to allow the Marcher Lords a free hand in such enterprises.

In such a climate deeds of cold expediency and ruthless cruelty were common, deeds that might have tortured a tender conscience and, at least, made many a powerful lord wonder whether his place in paradise could be safely assumed. One means of tempering the heinousness of their sins was to establish the rule of God, according to the Norman gospel, along with their massive castles and earthworks. This could be done through adopting local churches, granting lands to the abbeys of their home towns in Normandy or establishing new monastic institutions under the aegis of religious houses in England. Whilst powerful men saw the little monasteries that resulted from this as a tribute to God by which their souls might be saved the Welsh saw the matter in a different light. To them the new monasteries were the other face of the Norman conquerors, a body of men who were seen to be parsimonious with such New Testament ideas as love, meekness and gentleness of spirit. Nowhere could a priory be established away from the protection of a castle and therefore the two institutions of military and religious power had a certain identity, equally reviled by the Welsh. The priories automatically became houses of French or English monks that excluded the Welsh. This exclusion probably deepened the resentment felt by the latter.

The earliest and most successful Norman advances into Wales were generated from the southern march, from Chepstow north to Montgomery. From this area attacks were launched into Glamorgan, Brecon and the small princedoms of mid Wales. In military terms this was the soft underbelly. It quickly fell prey to the marauders, from Aberystwyth southwards the Normans held rule. In the space of a few decades castles were established at every key point and under their protective shadow the monasteries sprang up. These were established through grants of land to various Benedictine abbeys for the Benedictines were, initially, the only active order to whom such grants could be made. Clearly, when such a grant was made, the grantor intended that some sort of monastic institution should be established but it was the recipient abbot who decided just how that grant should be used. A reasonable grant of land in an advantageous site normally would be used to establish a priory. Such was the case at Chepstow, Monmouth, Abergavenny, Brecon, Pembroke,

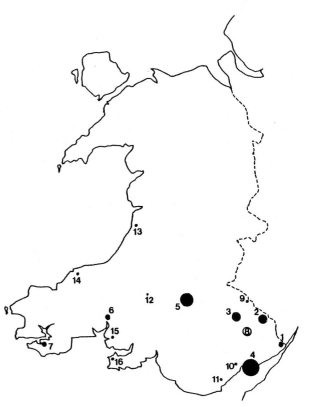

Size of houses as valued in 1291

Priory cells of insignificant value

Priories valued £0–£50

Priories valued £51–£100

Priories valued £101–£150

Priories valued £150+

Note that all houses are in the Norman controlled area of South Wales, Llanbadarn Fawr (13) survived only a few years.

Goldcliff and Ewenny. These were all conventual priories, being sufficient to support a full convent of monks through the endowments granted in the original gift. Ewenny was the only priory established away from its mother castle of Ogmore. This was because William de Londres, the patron, had included the local church in the original grant. Feeling uncomfortably exposed to hostile forces the priory had its own defensive arrangements which largely survive to this day.

Less substantial grants led to the recipient abbeys establishing a priory cell. This did not require that a full convent be supported but

Ewenny Priory.

just a prior and one or two monks. Some conventual buildings would exist to meet their needs but nothing as substantial as might be expected in a proper priory. Such establishments were to be found at Llangua near Abergavenny, remote Llandovery, Cardiff, Bassaleg near Newport, Llangennith at the wild end of the Gower pensinsula, Cardigan and Kidwelly. The most northerly of these Benedictine cells was at Llanbadarn Fawr, close to Aberystwyth. Here, for a few years, the Black Monks took over the famous Welsh monastery that had existed for centuries before being sent back to Gloucester by the natives. The purpose of these small cells, in an economic sense, was to gather the revenues of lands granted to the mother house. These mother houses also found the cells useful for dispersing the more maverick members of their convents. In a remote priory at the end of a distant peninsula a prior could be all but forgotten. If his behaviour was irregular it would lead astray very few monks.

No Benedictine priory in Wales ever achieved the status of abbey, they were all too small,

too poor, too remote and in a hostile land. Many of the priories had added difficulties in that they belonged directly to a French abbey. The fact that these priories had convents elected by a French mother house became a serious anomaly once political relations between England and France began to deteriorate. These priories became known as alien priories. Abergavenny, Chepstow, Goldcliff and Pembroke came into this category. In addition Llangua and Llangennith were alien cells.

The Benedictine churches were small compared with their counterparts in England, being, mostly, simple, cruciform buildings of modest length. To the Welsh, however, they were impressive structures with their massive piers, broad arcades and sturdy towers. The geometric patterning that adorned the doorways was not of the same spirit that produced the flowing, continuous, naturistic designs loved by the Celts. The new buildings may well have been viewed with the same hostility that we reserve for modern buildings that do not seem in tune with their

15

environment. Even the Saxons had reservations about the size of the new churches. They felt a fond conservatism for the small, homely structures that had served their forefathers.

The Reform Movement

After the first two decades of the 12th century the Benedictine priories were largely established alongside the foci of Norman power centres. But even as these priories were being founded new reform movements were developing on the continent and establishing themselves in Wales. The Benedictines, like all such religious movements, were inexorably caught up in an evolutionary process that began with religious fervour and strict observation of their rule but gradually slipped into decline and laxity. They were wealthy, and this bred a more relaxed and materialistic attitude amongst the monks of the convents. In Wales there was little opportunity to show the benefits of their religious practices to a population that was deeply hostile and, as events turned out, still at war with that earthly power that sustained the Benedictine houses. In Wales, then, the Benedictines had little prospect of success. In any case, the Welsh were largely debarred from entering the convents. Beleaguered and unpopular, some of the houses (Carmarthen, Llandovery and Llanbadarn Fawr) only survived a few years. When new monastic orders entered Wales it was not so much as reforming orders that they succeeded but as orders that were not so closely identified with the oppression of foreign military rule.

Among the first of these reforming orders to arrive in Wales was that originating from the Abbey of Tiron in northern France (some 25 miles south-west of Chartres). Monks from this abbey of reformed Benedictine order came to West Wales in 1115 at the instigation of Martin of Tiron who had become the Lord of Cemais. Martin's son, Robert, was particularly active in seeing that the monks were established in a new house at St Dogmael's near Cardigan. The site was close to that of an old Celtic religious house and sufficiently distant from the Norman fortifications of Cardigan for the conqueror's stigma not to attach to it. Shortly, a daughter house was founded on Caldey island, a site of another

● *Norman foundations*

• *Celtic houses adopting the Order*

✱ *Order of Tiron*

○ *Cluniac Cell*

✳ *Premonstratensian Abbey*

Key:
1. Llanthony	8. Penmon and Puffin Island
2. Carmarthen	9. St Dogmael's
3. Haverfordwest	10. Pill
4. St Kynemark	11. Caldey
5. Bardsey	12. St Clear's
6. St Tudwals	13. Malpas
7. Beddgelert	14. Talley

Celtic monastery. St Dogmael's was raised to the status of an abbey and, finally, a priory was founded for the order at Pill, near Milford Haven.

Another reforming order that reached South Wales at this time was that of the Augustinians. Because the convents of Augustinian houses were entirely comprised of priests the monks were known as canons. Although organised along strict monastic lines the Augustinian priories closely resembled some aspects of the old Celtic 'clas' churches which served a wide area through the offices of their priests. The resemblance was not such as would make the Welsh flock to their cause and at first there were few houses of the order. Llanthony, on the border of Wales, was essentially an English foundation established in 1108 and remained, to all intents and purposes, outside the province of Welsh influence. The Benedictine cell at Carmarthen was a foundation of Henry I that was not born to succeed but, reconstituted by the Bishop of St Davids as an Augustinian convent, it went on in later years to be among the most successful monastic houses in Wales. The Augustinian priory at Haverfordwest appears to date from rather later in the 12th century.

So far it is apparent that the early history of medieval monasteries in Wales is wholly connected with the influence of the Normans and the province of their influence - South Wales. This was due, as we have seen, to the political and military realities of the time and also to the fact that the continental styles of monasticism presented to the Welsh seemed almost inimical to them. The monasteries that existed in North Wales at the time, such as Penmon, Beddgelert and Bardsey, were wholly Welsh in origin and spirit. For the moment there was no possibility of Benedictines or Augustinians establishing houses of their orders without the support of a military presence.

A new and dynamic order, however, was beginning to arrive in Britain from France. The Cistercians were the most thoroughgoing in their zeal for reform, their desire for a simpler and anti-materialistic life, their dedication to the devotional aspects of the order and their emphasis on the merits of manual labour. Even more important, from the Welsh point of view, was their insistence on establishing houses in places remote from towns and castles, consciously independent of secular life and power. The abbeys were answerable only to the mother house, an allegiance that was reasonably free from political constraints. In spite of this the White Monks (known as such because of their dress) did not make an immediate impression on the Welsh. Three early monasteries founded between 1130 and 1131 (Neath, Basingwerk and Tintern) were, as far as the Welsh were concerned, perceptibly Norman in origin and affinity. Two of these houses were of the order of Savigny which only later merged with the Cistercians on account of the similarity of the two orders. Monks from Savigny had the same genesis as those from the abbey of Tiron. The

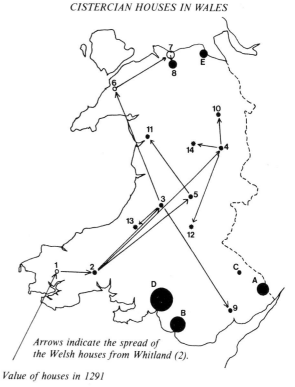

Arrows indicate the spread of the Welsh houses from Whitland (2).

Value of houses in 1291

- • £0–£50
- ● £51–£100
- ● £101–£150
- ● £151–£200
- ● £200+

Key:

1. Treffgarn (initial settlement before Whitland)	10. Valle Crucis
	11. Cymer
	12. Llansantffraed in Elfael
2. Whitland	13. Llanllyr
3. Strata Florida	14. Llanllugan
4. Strata Marcella	A. Tintern
5. Cwm Hir	B. Margam
6. Rhedynog Felen	C. Grace Dieu
7. Conway I	D. Neath
8. Conway II (Maenan)	E. Basingwerk
9. Llantarnam	

third house, Tintern, was one of the earliest Cistercian houses established in Britain but its relatively close proximity to that axial point of Norman power in South Wales, Chepstow, did not endear it to the Welsh. It was not until 1140 that a Cistercian house established itself in Wales that was sufficiently removed from Norman influence as to appeal strongly to the native population. Whitland was established by the great and powerful French house of Clairvaux and, as soon as it had found its permanent home,

17

achieved some success. Whitland was closer to the independent territories of Wales and the political and military climate was soon to favour its expansion northwards. In 1143 Maredudd, ruler of Maelienydd, approached the abbey to establish a monastery in the remote hills of his lordship in mid Wales. This early venture does not appear to have been favoured with success. It was more than 20 years before a similar venture was attempted - this time under Norman patronage in 1164. Robert FitzStephen invited Whitland to establish an abbey at Strata Florida in mid Wales. As this was taking place there was an abrupt and significant change in the power structure governing Wales. Rhys ap Gruffydd, the Lord Rhys, through a series of adroit military and political manoeuvres, established himself as the ruler of the greater part of South Wales. He immediately took upon himself the patronage of both Whitland and Strata Florida, the latter subsequently grew to have immense prestige. Over the next 40 years the Cistercian houses spread and flourished in Wales and became distinctly Welsh in character. Whitland was able to foster a new house in Powys called Strata Marcella and also refounded Maredudd's abbey at Cwmhir in Maelienydd. Strata Florida sent monks to Llantarnam in the extreme south east of Wales

in 1179 and later founded a significant house in North Wales. Initially settling near Caernarvon the monks moved on to Conway and became closely involved with the power at the heart of Welsh independence - Llywelyn the Great.

In South Wales the Lord Rhys himself founded a new abbey at Talley in 1184 but this was not of the Cistercian order as one might have expected. Talley belonged to the reformed Augustinian order of Premontre, an order that naturally recommended itself to Welshmen like Rhys because of its affinity to the traditional 'clas' monasticism. As in the Augustinian order, every member of the convent was a canon or an ordained priest and the abbey could therefore serve the surrounding area through its churches. The Premonstratensians, as they were known, had the further advantage of a greater simplicity of life, a great determination to get back to the original monastic ideal that made them comparable to the Cistercians. Like them, they wore a white habit and became known as White Canons.

At this point mention should be made of two houses founded in the reduced areas of Norman control. These were at Malpas near Newport and at St Clears, founded about 1120 and 1150 respectively. They were small cells belonging to houses of the great reformed order

Malpas Church. Copy of 19th century drawing of the priory church viewed from the south west.

that originated in the abbey of Cluny. By the time these two cells were established, however, the Cluniac order, like so many others, was already entering something of an evolutionary decline.

The Welsh Wars

In the last hundred years of Welsh independence the story of Welsh monasticism became inextricably involved with politics. In this respect the history of the abbeys and priories of Wales is rather different from that of their English equivalents whose development was not hindered by an apocalyptic struggle of the kind that took place in Wales. For the Welsh, certain houses were identified with their culture and became storehouses of literature and learning. Other houses became symbols of foreign influence and suffered accordingly in spite of the fact that they, too, were sometimes of cultural importance to the Welsh.

When the power of the Lord Rhys passed away a new power was rising in North Wales in the form of Llywelyn ap Owain, known to later generations as Llywelyn the Great. He had a fine understanding of the political realities of his day and established his hold on most of Wales in such a way as not to exceed his ability to maintain it. After his death in 1240 there was a short pause before his grandson, Llywelyn ap Gruffydd, assumed power. He attempted to restore to himself the territory of Llywelyn ap Owain but failed because his adversary, Edward I, was quite determined to put an end to Welsh independence. Llywelyn did not have the political adroitness of his forebear and, in the end, this seems to have helped Edward's cause. When Llywelyn fell in battle in 1282, near Builth in mid Wales, it marked the end of a conflict that for the Welsh was war but for the English was a mere series of campaigns. During these wars very considerable damage was done to the structures of Welsh life, particularly to the land itself which was frequently devastated. The religious houses of all orders suffered through the destruction of their buildings and also their lands which were a major source of revenue.

By the end of the 12th century the impetus that saw the foundation of 12 abbeys, 13 priories and eight priory cells in Wales was abating. Included in these houses was the great South Wales abbey of Margam which was founded from Clairvaux (Cistercian) in 1147 and became renowned as the richest house in Wales. Two more Cistercian houses were founded towards the end of the century. Near Dolgellau monks of Cwmhir established a house at Cymer in 1198 whilst the monks of Strata Marcella built a new abbey at Valle Crucis near Llangollen in 1201. These were not quite the last Cistercian ventures in Wales. In 1226 a final and rather forlorn abbey was established near Monmouth and called 'Grace Dieu'. It suffered enormous material damage during the wars of the 13th century. Three houses of Cistercian nuns were also established but the first was, unfortunately, scandalised by the lecherous attentions of its founder, the Abbot Enoch of Strata Marcella. The nunnery, which was at Llansantffraed in Elfael near Builth, apparently dissolved itself as a result (c.1174). Later nunneries at Llanllyr in the Aeron valley near Lampeter and at Llanllugan north of Newtown proved more enduring though never large. In the Norman province of South Wales there was one house for nuns at Usk, predictably of the Benedictine order.

In North Wales the Cistercian order, principally at Conway, flourished under the Welsh rulers who liberally endowed the houses with lands. Such was the wealth of Conway, contrasted with the little Welsh monastery of Beddgelert, that the latter was in danger of being taken over by its powerful neighbour. Apparently with an eye to self protection, Beddgelert aligned itself with the Augustinian order - a natural move for its ordained monks to continue in their more or less traditional way of life. It seems that the other Welsh houses of North Wales took the same course at this time. By the mid 13th century Penmon, Bardsey, St Tudwals and Beddgelert were all priories of the Augustinian order.

In South Wales a very different course of events was taking place. Here the political uncertainty was greater and the changes of power more frequent as the Welsh princes and the marcher lords wrested power from each other. The Welsh Cistercian houses suffered from retaliations and invasions. The hotbeds of Welsh nationalism, Whitland and Llantarnam, were both victims of the unrest. Whitland Abbey was actually attacked by the Normans. Llantarnam was financially crippled by the powerful de Clare family. On the other hand Neath and Margam Abbeys both suffered considerable material damage at the hands of the

Welsh whilst Grace Dieu was completely destroyed by Llywelyn in 1223. King John actually ordered the destruction of both Strata Florida and Cwmhir on separate occasions because they were so openly hostile to him. Such was the climate of unrest that some small cells closed down. The monks at Cardiff were withdrawn to their mother church at Tewkesbury. Bassaleg was farmed or rented out. Benedictine priories outside the protection of the town walls were particularly at risk. In 1223 Kidwelly Priory was burned to the ground and it seems unthinkable that Abegavenny Priory escaped the frequent attention that the Welsh paid to the town.

As the struggle reached further into the Welsh heartland the monastic houses of North Wales also began to suffer. In the final upheaval of 1282 little Penmon was burnt and Conway suffered severely. And yet, during this turbulent period, the Welsh abbeys and priories managed to fulfil much of the early optimism that must have accompanied their foundation. The Cistercian abbeys, in particular, wrought enormous changes in Wales through their agricultural conquest of this unpromising land. Leland, after the Dissolution, credited Strata Florida with having changed the face of much of mid Wales through the destruction of the forests for sheep walks. Most Cistercian houses had vast flocks of sheep which were a major source of income. There can be no doubt that an abbey like Strata Florida, rather like a modern factory, was a source of economic energy in the empty heart of Wales. Originally there would have been a substantial number of lay brethren and many other people with business to conduct with the abbey. The status of the abbeys was further increased by the fact that royalty associated freely with them. The Cistercian houses became repositories of the cultural and artistic efforts of a large part of the population. Their buildings, although meant to be austere, were far above anything that the native Welsh had seen before. Rare indications, such as the west door of Strata Florida Abbey, suggest that the Welsh Cistercian houses were more in tune with the Celtic genius for design than the Benedictines. Fine masonry, weather-proof roofs, enormous size, sanitation, rooms for warming, the attractions of such places must have seemed endless at the material level alone. The austere conventual life had its compensations in relative security, regular

Detail of the Keystone
West Door
Strata Florida

After an illustration in S. Williams'
'The Cistercian Abbey of Strata Florida' 1889.

diet and the sure knowledge of a better life in the hereafter. Not everything was perfect, however, and Gerald Cambrensis, in his tours of Wales at the end of the 12th century, reveals some of the less attractive aspects of monastic life. He had suffered at the hands of the Cistercians who had a bad reputation for astuteness and avarice. Strata Florida had relieved Gerald of his treasured library and he never forgot this. Gerald criticised several other abbeys for their uncharitable behaviour but the greed of Abbot Peter of Whitland met with his special disapproval. The feud that took place between Whitland and Talley brought disgrace to the former but was not, unfortunately, a singular occurrence. After the Welsh wars there were further examples of outright conflict involving other Cistercian houses. Compared with the Benedictines, however, Gerald regarded the Cistercians as paragons of seemliness. Surely there was some prejudice behind his criticisms and yet there is the unmistakable impression that the moral degeneracy that marked the Benedictine houses in Wales a century later was already making itself apparent at the end of the 12th century. Perhaps the Norman spirit of freebooting conquest demanded a degree of cynicism from those who gave it moral authority.

After defeat

In an intensely religious age the defeat of the Welsh must have presented a spiritual and moral crisis. The monks who sadly carried Llywelyn ap Gruffydd's headless body from the banks of the Irfon to their remote abbey in the hills at Cwmhir must surely have talked and meditated on their past and future. Their prayers and hopes unfulfilled, God had judged against them. To them this was not just another sordid episode in a struggle that was always hopeless, their house had long been committed to the Welsh cause and had suffered on its account. If those same monks had any knowledge of the appalling moral state that was to be found in the religious houses of the 'enemy' in South Wales then their sense of the injustice of events would have been doubled. Our own knowledge of that moral condition is due largely to a visitation made by Archbishop Pecham in 1284 to the monasteries of South Wales. Other records reveal that the irregularities that he found were by no means isolated instances. The prior of Pembroke was deposed for being incontinent and a disgrace to the order, the prior of Kidwelly similarly revealed 'manifest faults'. The prior at the important house of Brecon was accused of being a liar, a fraud, a drunkard and a lecher. Such leadership undoubtedly had an effect on the whole convent as could be seen at Abergavenny where, in the 14th century, the monks could be seen chatting and gambling when they should have been at prayers. The townsfolk were aware that loose women consorted with the monks whilst the chief culprit, Prior Fulk Gastard, absconded with the priory valuables when it was apparent that such goings-on would no longer be tolerated.

Unfortunately, such decadence was not confined to Benedictine houses and even extended to some Welsh convents. Haverfordwest Priory had certainly let strict standards decline though not to the extent indicated at Pembroke and Brecon. Llanthony also had its problems, largely due to bad relations between the prior and the canons. At Talley the canons were said to keep their mistresses openly and the abbey was put under the supervision of the English Premonstratensian house of Welbeck. There is a suspicion, however, that Welsh houses were criticised for ulterior motives. By suggesting that Welsh convents needed new leadership English influence might be more easily introduced. The influence of Whitland, which was deeply nationalistic, was a problem for the English and pretexts were sought to extricate abbeys from that association. This may have been the case at Talley and also at Strata Marcella which was put under the control of Buildwas near Shrewsbury.

With defeat came the abandonment of ambition for many Welsh houses. Abbeys like Cymer and Cwmhir gave up trying to complete their churches which remained without transepts or presbyteries of the normal pattern. Talley left its nave largely unfinished. Many other Cistercian houses remained noticeably unchanged during the period after the wars while others were rebuilding on an ambitious scale. Strata Florida, Strata Marcella, Valle Crucis, Whitland and Basingwerk all retained their twelfth-century churches. But Conway was rebuilt on a new site at the expense of Edward I. It was in a new style with aisles on either side of the presbytery. The most Strata Florida could afford was to lengthen its presbytery a little. But in the south the old 'Norman' abbeys of Neath and Tintern were rebuilt in new and magnificent style. Margam had already built a presbytery in the new style together with a chapter house of great beauty. Benedictine priories like Brecon and Kidwelly were able to make substantial alterations and additions. The Augustinian house at Haverfordwest made various additions to the conventual buildings that added to the comfort of the place. This was all quite a contrast to the conquered areas further north. Almost a memorial to lost hope, the monks at Cymer built a little tower at the west end of their nave because they would, now, never have a handsome crossing tower at the heart of their projected church.

It would be wrong, however, to suggest that even the most extensive rebuilding at this time was a reflection of new prosperity. It was more an expression of a new spirit, for all the monastic houses now entered a period of extreme financial difficulty from which they never really recovered. Expensive building work such as that at Neath was an extra burden on the abbey's coffers that it could ill afford. Revenues from the monasteries' lands were reduced because of the destruction wrought by the wars yet the crown was seeking to realise money from these nominally wealthy establishments through taxation. The waves of benefactions that enriched the houses in their early years were now receding, local disturb-

Cymer Abbey. The west end of the nave with the base of the west tower on the left.

ances continued, all around there was little source of economic comfort for a hard pressed prior or abbot.

For the alien priories there was no relief after the wars for it was at this time that England launched into its long conflict with France. The alien priories were all subject to French abbeys and naturally were viewed with a mixture of resentment and suspicion. The resentment was felt because the French abbeys could draw revenue from Britain through such houses, the suspicion was that reserved for enemies in one's midst. Special suspicion rested on those houses near the sea and these were subject to extra restrictions. In Wales there were five alien priories and a further four alien cells. Of these nine houses all but two were close to the sea and five were actually in ports. So it was that a substantial number of Welsh Benedictine houses and the two Cluniac cells lost much of their revenue and were harassed in various other ways for over a century. They were all finally sup-

pressed at the beginning of the 15th century.

If there was hope that, over the passage of years, better times would come for the abbeys and priories of Wales then it was a forlorn hope. The middle of the 14th century was marked by that great curse of Europe, the Black Death. Although remote from the European heartland, Wales was in no degree spared the effects of the plague. Many Welsh convents lost brethren during the course of the plague which sorely affected the strength of the houses. It also left the houses unable to work their own lands, a weakness particularly felt by the Cistercian houses which initially depended on large numbers of lay brethren to work the land. After the Black Death there was an increasing tendency to farm the possessions of the religious houses. The word 'farm' here indicates that properties were rented out and the revenue that came from the property was derived from rents alone. Whilst this relieved a house of the problem of working a given property the income was, naturally, greatly diminished.

The 14th century saw itself out with one final catastrophe for Wales. Owain Glyndwr's rebellion was, at first, a small affair. By the time it had run its course, however, it had taken in all Wales and, for a time, united the country as an independent nation. The flame of independence flared for a little time, spluttered and finally went out almost of its own accord. During that short interval many monastic houses were deeply affected. Some, like Whitland and Llantarnam, threw their lot in with the Welsh cause and were duly penalised. Llantarnam's abbot was actually killed in battle not far from the abbey. Others, like Conway, wavered before finally coming in on the Welsh side. They suffered less. One abbey, Cwmhir, never recovered from the period. Leland tells us that it was "spoiled and defaced" in the rebellion and probably remained that way until the Dissolution. Strata Marcella was also damaged and repairs to Valle Crucis at the time suggest that the buildings there were damaged during the conflict. Strata Florida might

have been a source of strength to the Welsh had it not been that a military garrison was placed in the abbey. One assumes that the abbey far from benefited from this association. Margam, Abergavenny, Llanthony and Carmarthen are all known to have suffered damage. Other houses, too, may have suffered without any record surviving. Even those houses that escaped immediate physical damage suffered on account of their lands being pillaged with the consequent loss of revenues.

The last century of monasticism

Early in the 15th century the misery of one group of religious houses was ended. All alien priories were dissolved since their position had become quite untenable. Most, such as Monmouth and Abergavenny whose apports (or rents) were simply diverted away from their French mother houses to English counterparts, emerged as thoroughly English houses. By various arrangements Chepstow and Pembroke

The twelve-sided chapter house at Margam.

23

survived but Goldcliff was closed. The priory buildings at Goldcliff were, in any case, being ruined by the inroads of the sea. The cells of Llangua, Llangennith and St Clears also ceased to have any conventual life.

The final century of monasticism was marked by a general decline in most aspects of conventual life. Llanthony Priory, once the favoured house of the royalty of England, became a mere cell of Gloucester's Augustinian priory. Other houses suffered from serious mismanagement which left their finances in a parlous state. Goldcliff had been a victim of imprudent housekeeping. Talley, Cymer and Whitland are also known to have suffered in this way. The problem may well have been far more widespread since there is ample evidence of the indifference of the priors and abbots to the well-being of their houses. The prior of Penmon resided most of the time in nearby Beaumaris where he may even have kept a wife. The abbot of Basingwerk is known to have breached the vow of celibacy in the final years before the Dissolution. He, like the abbot of Strata Marcella, had also been astute in increasing his own wealth from the abbey's resources. In Neath the abbot provided himself with more spacious apartments by taking up some of the room used by the monks. Most convents were greatly reduced in number and fewer buildings were needed for them. This was surely the case in Valle Crucis where the abbot was able to establish his quarters in the most convenient part of the monks' dormitory.

Further evidence of the reduced strength of the convents comes from the known decline of the buildings. In Strata Florida the south range was already in ruins before the Dissolution. The monks presumably used one of the other wings for their infirmary and refectory. Cwmhir, Strata Marcella, Whitland masonry for re-use in other buildings. Where not one stone is left on another today those stones may frequently be found in neighbouring farms, houses or churches. Cwmhir is a fine example, falling into ruins before the Dissolution, its finest feature may well have been its splendid 14-arched, thirteenth-century arcade. Six of these arches were taken to Llandiloes for use in the town church. It is apparent that some houses, such as Strata Marcella and Conway, were dismantled with extraordinary haste. There are virtually no remains of five of the Cistercian houses.

Benedictine houses fared rather better because their naves were used as parish churches. Some of the churches have survived almost intact, though sometimes rather heavily restored. Brecon, Abergavenny and Ewenny are fairly complete examples. Some of the churches of priory cells have also survived fairly well, notably at Llangennith and Kidwelly. Unfortunately there was rarely seen to be a need to preserve any part of the conventual buildings of these priories and sometimes even the monastic portion of the church was demolished as well. Townsfolk might simply build a wall across the eastern end of their nave and allow the monk's portion of the church to go to ruin. This happened at Pembroke, Monmouth and Chepstow.

Of the Augustinian priory churches only Beddgelert and Penmon remained in use. The Cluniac churches of Malpas and St Clears also survived but Malpas fell victim to nineteenth-century rebuilding. The church of Talley Abbey also remained in use for a while before a new and smaller church was erected nearby. St Dogmaels church also survived in use for some time but was finally abandoned.

Of the conventual buildings of the monasteries even less survives. Those of the Benedictine houses were almost entirely destroyed, the best survival being the famous oriel window in Monmouth - Geoffrey's Window. More complete remains are found of those and Basingwerk were also in very poor condition. Not only the Cistercian houses were falling down. Monmouth Priory was in an appalling condition and Beddgelert had been ruined by fire. In the days of their greatness the magnificent buildings of the monasteries had been their glory, now they were a drain on the revenues of the hard pressed convents. In some cases houses could afford modest building works. Margam, which had been left quite ruinous after the Glyndwr rebellion, was restored in the middle of the 15th century. Conway was in a poor condition but the abbot, Dafydd ap Owain, carried out the necessary repairs and rebuilding. The little priory at Pill was noted, in 1504, to be in good condition and recently restored. Carmarthen had been sacked during the Glyndwr rebellion but seems to have been maintained in good condition in the period before the Dissolution. Some houses even managed new works. At Tintern, wealthiest of Welsh houses, the infirmary was substantially restructured.

Geoffrey's window – Monmouth Priory.

Little Penmon Priory managed a new warming house and kitchen, St Dogmael's built a new guest house by the west range and rebuilt, in rather splendid style, the north transept of its church, even the decaying Strata Florida has evidence of some modest work in its cloister garth.

The later history of the North Wales Cistercian abbeys is marred by the conflict surrounding the former abbot of Conway, John ap Rhys. His altercation with Strata Florida, which was conducted from both Conway and Cymer, brought financial ruin and lasting shame to the houses involved. It may be that they were pawns in a wider political game but the impression that these Welsh houses were in a self destructive spiral is all too strong.

For most Welsh houses the Dissolution under Henry VIII took place between 1535 and 1539. As can be seen from the above account, most houses were in a pitiful state by that time and becoming more ruinous by the year. Some special provision would have been required to support them and that was hardly likely to be forthcoming in the prevailing political climate. At the Dissolution the Cistercian houses were, in many cases, quickly dismantled. Lead was stripped from roofs and the ancient timbers used to melt the lead. Bells were carted away together with the best parts of the masonry for re-use in other buildings. Where not one stone is left on another today those stones may frequently be found in neighbouring farms, houses or churches. Cwmhir is a fine example, falling into ruins before the Dissolution, its finest feature may well have been its splendid 14-arched, thirteenth-century arcade. Six of these arches were taken to Llanidloes for use in the town church. It is apparent that some houses, such as Strata Marcella and Conway, were dismantled with extraordinary haste. There are virtually no remains of five of the Cistercian houses. Benedictine houses fared rather better because their naves were used as parish churches. Some of the churches have survived almost intact, though sometimes rather heavily restored. Brecon, Abergavenny and Ewenny are fairly complete examples. Some of the churches of priory cells have also survived fairly well, notably at Llangennith and Kidwelly. Unfortunately there was rarely seen to be a need to preserve any part of the conventual buildings of these priories and sometimes even the monastic portion of the church was demolished as well. Townsfolk might simply build a wall across the eastern end of their nave and allow the monks' portion of the church to go to ruin. This happened at Pembroke, Monmouth and Chepstow.

Of the Augustinian priory churches only Beddgelert and Penmon remained in use. The Cluniac churches of Malpas and St Clears also survived but Malpas fell victim to nineteenth-century rebuilding. The church of Talley Abbey also remained in use for a while before a new and smaller church was erected nearby. St Dogmaels church also survived in use for some time but was finally abandoned.

Of the conventual buildings of the monasteries even less survives. Those of the Benedictine houses were almost entirely destroyed, the best survival being the famous oriel window in Monmouth - 'Geoffrey's Window'. More complete remains are found of those houses built far from urban land pressures. The most complete of these are undoubtedly of the Cistercian houses of Tintern and Valle Crucis but there are notable remains at Neath and Basingwerk. In all, just enough survives of the abbeys and priories of Wales to give a fair impression of the zenith of monasticism in the country in the Middle Ages.

Further reading

F.G. Cowley, *The Monastic Order in South Wales 1066-1349*. Cardiff 1977. The definitive account of the subject.

D. Knowles and R.N. Hadcock, *Medieval Religious Houses of England and Wales* (2nd edition) 1971.

D.H. Williams, *The Welsh Cistercians*. Caldey Island 1984. In two volumes. Leaves no stone unturned.

G. Williams, *The Welsh Church from Conquest to Reformation*. Cardiff 1962.

Part II

THE ABBEYS AND PRIORIES

The buildings

The buildings of any abbey or priory served two purposes. One purpose was to provide for the accommodation of the convent, the other to provide for its worship. The buildings, therefore, divided into two parts, the church and the conventual buildings. Of these the church was the most important, the *raison d'être* of the monastery. The church reflected the strength and wealth of the community, its liturgical needs, cultural and political achievements. Naturally the most important monastic houses tended to build the most impressive churches. Through these churches we discern a great deal about the life of the convent. The plan of the church developed to meet the needs of the convent and any other people who might use it. In some cases, particularly in Cistercian abbeys, the church had to accommodate the requirements of sophisticated ceremonies through various entrances and passages but in some cases it is clear that the ceremonial life of the convent was restricted, perhaps impaired, by the limitation of the design of the church. Cymer and Cwmhir Abbeys provide good examples of this.

The simplest plan for any monastic church is a simple hall structure with no elaboration of any kind. It may be that in some cases such a building was initially erected for the use of the convent and subsequently replaced or enlarged. Llanllugan, a tiny and remote church that was used by a nearby convent of Cistercian nuns, is such a building.

The Benedictine monks shared the use of their churches with the inhabitants of the towns in which they were placed. Their main requirement was that they could continue with their own worship unhindered by the parishioners. A stone screen or pulpitum, such as survives at Ewenny, was the solution to the problem of separating secular from monastic uses of the church and it was normal for the Benedictines to occupy the east end of the building where they could be unobserved by the parishioners. At the Dissolution the parishioners frequently tore down the monastic end of the church with some alacrity but occasionally these east ends survived as the chancel of the new church. At Pembroke the present chancel, which used to be the monks' church, was in ruins until restored at the beginning of this century but at Abergavenny it has survived the passage of the years reasonably intact. In the case of the priory cells in Wales the nave-with-chancel plan was normal and in all the surviving examples a tower was added at the west end or, at Llangennith, beside the middle part of the church.

The cruciform church plan was typically adopted by all the orders of monks and allowed for greater complexitiy of ceremonies and worship. The crossing of the cruciform church was usually the point at which a tower was built although the Cistercians tended to frown on this elaboration. At Whitland the tower was probably never built and elsewhere the Cistercian churches tended to be restrained in the height of this 'crossing' tower. Most of the great Benedictine churches were of the cruciform pattern with notable survivals at Brecon and Abergavenny. The Benedictine Order of Tiron and the Augustinians also favoured this plan which was adopted at St Dogmaels, Carmarthen and Haverfordwest and Pill. The addition of chapels in the east wall of the transept allowed for the accommodation of additional altars. At Brecon these chapels have survived in part and at Ewenny their size and position can be clearly seen.

It will be noticed that the Cistercian churches are, as yet, hardly mentioned in this context. The requirements of Cistercian churches were somewhat different from those of most other orders. They were built entirely for the use of the abbey but would have to accommodate, especially in their early days, large numbers of lay brethren. These lay brethren, vital cogs in the machinery of the Order, worshipped in the nave section of the church to which they had peculiar access through their own doorway. The monks tended to separate this part of the church from the rest of the building by walling in the arcades between the nave and the side aisles. As a result their processions could pass the whole length of the church, along the aisles on either side of the nave, unobserved by the lay brethren. Remains of the walling in the bays of the arcades can be clearly seen at Strata Florida. The processional aisles, in some later churches extended either side of the presbytery and around the east end of the church. This arrangement can be seen at Neath and Tintern but a superb example survives intact just across the South Wales border at Abbey Dore, the mother house of little Grace Dieu Abbey.

Abergavenny Priory. Decoration on the monks' stalls.

The core of the church was in the presbytery and choir, for the monks it was a church within a church. The presbytery held the high altar, the choir contained the monks' stalls ranged in rows opposite each other for the antiphonal chanting of the offices. Only in the Benedictine priory of Abergavenny have these stalls survived in Wales but we know that normally they occupied the area beneath the crossing tower. At Basingwerk the pier supporting the arch of the crossing tower shows a recess which permitted the stalls to fit in the choir with an adequate intervening space.

Apart from the additional chapels the transepts allowed access to other parts of the monastic precinct, whilst one transept might lead to the cemetery the opposite transept led to the conventual buildings.

The conventual buildings

In the smallest priory cells the accommodation for monks was probably quite informal. There are no survivals in Wales of the conventual buildings attaching to a small cell but such indications as there are suggest that no particular pattern was followed. At Cardigan the monks entered the church through a small door in the south-east corner of the chancel. This may have been connected with the living accommodation to the south east by a short, covered walkway. At Kidwelly the conventual buildings were a little to the north and at St Clears somewhere to the south west. In the majority of abbeys and priories, however, the conventual buildings followed a more predictable plan following traditional practice and practical requirements. Where these varied from the normal it was usually on account of restrictions placed on the site by

29

Monks' entrance to Cardigan Priory — south-east corner of chancel.

factors such as steep slopes, rivers or crowded town conditions.

The monks usually chose to live on the sunny side of the church. A large church would cut off a substantial amount of light and warmth to a cloister on its north side but at Pembroke, Monmouth, Conway, Tintern and Caldey the monks chose this side of the church for their buildings. The reasons for this are not always clear but in some cases it would appear that the need for a fresh water drain flowing under the buildings dictated their position. In other cases the convent may have been seeking the quietest corner of a crowded site. At Monmouth the siting of the conventual buildings north of the church placed the monks well away from the bustle of town life but within the protection of the town enceinte.

It was normal to arrange the conventual buildings around a square cloister garth (enclosure) so that they enclosed three sides and the church enclosed the remaining side. The walk around the cloister was covered so that work could continue in adverse weather conditions. There are no remains of the covered walks in Welsh houses but many surviving buildings show signs of where the roof of the walkway attached. Holes for the roof timbers to fit in or stone sills to fit over the roof are often seen, at Valle Crucis both are in evidence.

The conventual buildings are usually called ranges: east, west and south or north as appropriate to their position around the cloister. Of these ranges the east was by far the most important because it contained the monks' principal office, the chapter house, and their sleeping quarters. The range was on two floors, the ground floor consisting of the chapter house with an elaborate doorway and windows either side. Between the chapter house and the transept of the church to which the east range attached there was usually a small room which could be used as a sacristy, a book room, a combination of these two or as a passage to the area beyond the range. On the other side of the chapter house the ground floor might hold a parlour and a warming house. In the Cistercian houses this space was often used to house the novices whilst the monks had their dormitory in the upper floor of the range. This would normally extend to a reredorter over the main drain. The monks required access to the church through two entrances, either of which would be used according to the time of day or night. For night offices the monks entered the church by a door leading directly from their dormitory into the adjacent transept of the church. This door led onto a flight of stairs which descended to the floor of the church. Where these stairs remain they are often the most evocative survivals from the monastic period but unfortunately this is very rare. In Wales the base of these stairs may sometimes be seen, at Neath there is an elegant stone handrail set in the wall of the transept above the base of the stairs. At Haverfordwest the stairs were contained within the thickness of the wall of the transept and at Ewenny they spiral up the south-west corner of the transept. During the daytime the monks left the dormitory by the day stairs at the other end of the room and then entered the church through a door next to the transept. This door was often an elaborate creation because it was so frequently used by the monks in their normal and ceremonial use of the church. The day stairs tend not to survive any better than the night stairs but at Basingwerk the first few steps remain intact. At Valle Crucis a rather cramped flight of day stairs remains intact, here they were built into the east range and enter the cloister walk by a small door next to the chapter house entrance.

The chapter house was always central to the east range. Here the daily running of the convent and its business were organised. Prayers and readings took place, confessions were made, punishments received before the rest of the monks. In architectural terms, also, the chapter house was pre-eminent among the conventual buildings. A simple chapter house such as that at Valle Crucis would be finely vaulted and windowed. Subtleties of design were introduced, at Llanthony the gradual narrowing of the room to the east would have enhanced the sense of length and height. The exquisite 12-sided chapter house at Margam is one of the high points of medieval architecture in Wales in spite of its present state of ruination. In some instances the stone benches along the walls for the monks to be seated whilst in chapter have survived.

The south range was principally taken up with the monks' dietary needs and consisted of a frater (the dining hall or refectory) with a kitchen close by. Early arrangements of the south range had a long frater with its main axis running east-west. This plan survived in many smaller houses throughout the life of the house but later Cistercian planning turned the frater round so that its narrow, gable end faced onto the cloister. This provided more space for the kitchen to be built into the range. There are some survivals of fraters but that at Basingwerk is particularly interesting with the remains of the reader's pulpit and the serving hatch from the kitchen still visible.

The kitchen was placed close to the frater for the simple reason that the food could remain warm in transit to the table. The kitchen was placed west of the frater so that, in Cistercian abbeys, the lay brothers of the west range could have the same facility for their own dining room. The lay brothers occupied much of the west range with their dormitory and frater in the same building. The range was shared with the cellarer's rooms and was busy with the more practical demands of the monastery's life, the bringing in of the victuals and the conduct of trade. To separate this secular wing from the rest of the ranges a lane was sometimes constructed with a wall on the east side against which the roof of the cloister walk might be

built away from the hustle and bustle of the west range. The silence of the cloister was thus preserved. At Neath we see remains of this arrangement whilst at Whitland there appears to have been a lane of exceptional width.

Some houses were able to provide special facilities for the aged and infirm members of the convent. At Tintern the infirmary building was a substantial structure with its own little cloister and special approach to the church. Unfortunately the only survival of an infirmary building in Wales above foundation level is at St Dogmael's but the remains there are quite substantial. The normal practice was to build the infirmary building towards the far end of the east range and to the east of it.

The abbot or prior naturally required his own special lodging in the monastery. This lodging normally related to the east range where the head of the house could oversee the life of the convent. At Tintern, where the conventual buildings were all to the north of the church, the abbot had a separate house in the northeast part of the precinct but at Neath and Valle Crucis the abbot ultimately adopted

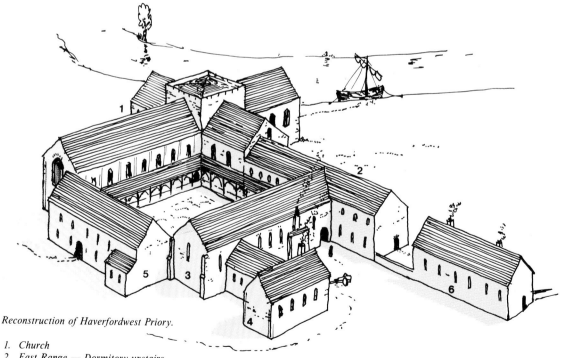

Reconstruction of Haverfordwest Priory.

1. *Church*
2. *East Range — Dormitory upstairs*
3. *Frater or Dining Area*
4. *Farmery*
5. *West Wing.*
6. *Infirmary*

part of the monks' dormitory for his own accommodation. It would seem that at Neath the abbot's apartments were, by the time of the Dissolution, of some magnificence. In non Cistercian houses the abbot or prior sometimes had his rooms in the west range above the cellarer's stores.

For visitors guest accommodation had to be provided. Houses such as Penmon, Cymer and Margam are known to have been used by the Crown or its officers on frequent occasions whilst visiting or passing through their locality. Offering hospitality to such people, as monastic houses were bound to do, could be a serious drain on finances. Guests were usually accommodated in rooms in the west range or adjacent to the west end of the church. There is evidence of such a building at St Dogmael's where a small building in this position has been interpreted as a guest house.

The entrance to the monastery precinct was through the gatehouse of which there are three surviving examples in Wales. At Neath one side of the gatehouse stands by the roadside, the pavement running along the line of the lane used by the abbey visitors. The gatehouse at Llanthony is a large barn-like building standing a little distance from the church across a field. At Usk the gatehouse to the Benedictine nunnery has survived quite intact and is one of the most complete and charming medieval buildings still standing in Wales.

Further reading

R. Gilyard-Beer. *Abbeys*. A short but comprehensive introduction to monastic buildings now in the care of English Heritage or Cadw.

F.H. Crossley, *The English Abbey*. Batsford. Out-of-print but fairly easily available from second-hand book shops, a charming and excellently illustrated account of the monastic houses of the country. In spite of its title there is considerable reference to Welsh houses.

The guide

The guide gives a brief introduction to each site and points out aspects of particular interest in the history and surviving remains of each building. In many cases, particularly where the site is in the hands of Cadw, excellent guides are available and these should be consulted if the site is to be fully enjoyed. Where such a guide is not available it is to be hoped that the notes in this book will be found helpful and illuminating.

Visitors who need quick reference to points of interest should note that the sections headed 'The buildings' are normally divided into two parts. The first part describes the original appearance of the church and conventual buildings whilst the latter half of the section examines the extant remains. The main illustration attempts to superimpose a reconstruction of the original buildings over the present remains. Certain conventions have been followed in these drawings. Dotted lines indicate a more speculative reconstruction, not based on real evidence but on comparison with similar models. At Cymer, Talley and Cwmhir the dotted lines indicate the monks' original intentions for the completed churches where

building programmes had to be abandoned. Covered cloister walks have not been reconstructed as these might confuse the drawings.

Visitors may be surprised to find some buildings depicted in the illustrations as ruins when they see before them well-built and complete churches. At Beddgelert, for example, the nineteenth-century church which is in normal use, occupies the site of the monastic church of the Augustinian canons. Parts of this church survive in the existing building and it is the remains of this church which are the sole subject of my illustration. Other churches which I have 'vandalised' in this way are Penmon, Margam, Monmouth, Chepstow, Abergavenny, Usk, Cardigan and St Clears.

In two cases, Caldey and Tintern, I have not superimposed the reconstruction of the original buildings for the simple reason that the drawing would become a confused mass of lines. In both cases a separate reconstruction is provided.

The large arrow on the drawings indicates the normal public approach to the building or the ruins when this approach is through a specific entrance. The smaller arrow on the drawings indicates the direction of north.

Abergavenny

History

Abergavenny dates from the earliest conquest of Wales when Hamelin de Balun began the castle, about 1090, and began to lay out the plan of the border town in the Usk valley at the very edge of the Welsh uplands. Outside the town walls, presumably some time before 1100, he founded the Benedictine priory of St Mary's. Initially it was a cell but by the time of Henry II, and before 1189, it became a fully conventual priory. It was a daughter house of St Vincent of Le Mans, in France. The east gate of Abergavenny which led to the priory became known as the 'Monk Gate'. Inside the town de Balun also built another church, St John's, which soon decayed.

Abergavenny was subject to frequent attacks by the Welsh, notably in 1172, 1176 and 1262. It is inconceivable that the priory, lying outside the protection of the town walls, escaped their attentions.

In 1291 the priory was valued at £51 and owned a modest 241 acres of estate. Although intended for a full convent of 12 monks and a prior there were only five monks in 1319. This was the time of a visitation due to reported breaches of conventual discipline. It was found that the five monks led a dissolute life, there was no silence in the cloister - indeed, when they should have been attending to divine office they were found to be playing dice. Worse still, they had been seen with loose women. We may ask, "Where was the prior - Fulk Gastard - in all this?" He was known to be guilty of considerable immorality and vanished

ABERGAVENNY

1. *Nave*
2. *Presbytery with monks' stalls*
3. *Entrance to Herbert Chapel*
4. *South transept site connecting with east range*
5. *South (frater) range*
6. *Possible reredorter suggested by Doorway in wall of east range*

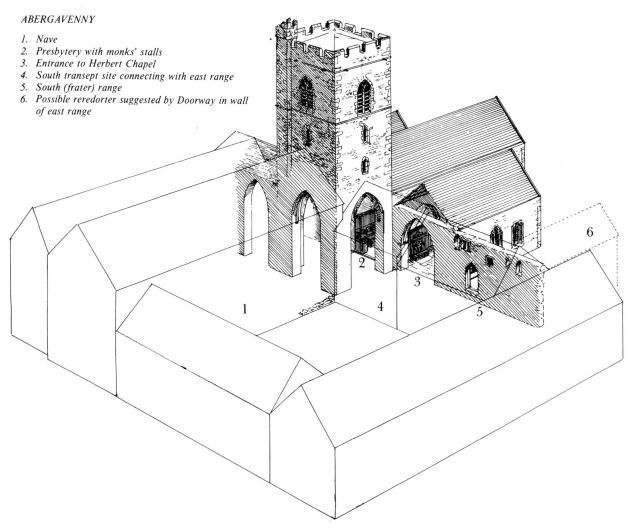

Abergavenny Priory. East wall of the south transept incorporating some remains from the east range of the conventual buildings.

before the visitation with a large quantity of the priory valuables.

Following the outbreak of war with France in 1294, Abergavenny was seized because it was an alien priory - directly owned by the French abbey of St Vincent. Control over the finances of the priory came under the Crown and this put great pressure on the convent.

In the final siege of the town by Glendower's rebels the priory suffered severely, being set on fire with books, ornaments and buildings destroyed.

In 1535, at the time of the Dissolution, the priory's income was valued at £129 and there were five monks in the convent. It was dissolved the following year.

The buildings

The Priory Church at Abergavenny, as we understand from the fourteenth-century shell of today, was a typical cruciform building with the monks' choir and presbytery at the east end. An aisle was added to the north side of the nave probably in the 14th century. This would have enlarged the space available for the secular use of the church. Each of the two transepts was enlarged by a chapel extending eastwards - these are now known as the Herbert and Lewis Chapels, south and north respectively. In these chapels, particularly the Herbert Chapel, were placed the remains of and monuments to the great patrons of the house and the Lords of Abergavenny. The conventual buildings apparently followed the normal plan completing a rectangle on the south side of the church adjoining the nave and transept. To the west of the west range, and parallel with it, was a large tithe barn for the use of the priory.

Of the original Norman church little survives today. The east window has re-used its original Norman arch but is otherwise of recent date. A notable survival is the Norman font which was recovered from the churchyard after centuries of misuse. In the 14th century the church was substantially rebuilt and much has survived from this period. In spite of some serious mutilations, particularly the replacement of the arcade in the nave, the spirit of the fourteenth-century rebuilding has survived. The present nave and north aisle are essentially a rebuilding of the late 19th century but the impression on entering the church from the west end is of a high, long and dignified building. This impression is created by the high pointed arches of the crossing where the lines have been faithfully preserved although the original fabric may be lacking in parts. The crossing tower is well preserved, an impressive structure from the outside. The north transept has been attenuated at some time whilst the south transept has been rebuilt. East of the crossing the building is altogether more authentic and the sense of this is heightened by the remarkable set of memorials surviving in the Herbert and Lewis Chapels. Taken together with the effigy in the nave, a superb carving of the 13th century, this is the most important set of memorials in Wales. The nave memorial referred to is thought to be of George de Canteloupe, a Lord of Abergavenny who died in 1273.

Of great importance are the splendid canopied choir stalls of the late 15th century. These could seat 24 monks and are a unique survival among the abbeys and priories of Wales. The prior's seat is raised with a mitre over it.

Of the conventual buildings there are no real survivals but many clues. The area they once occupied is now delineated by the walls of the small car park on the south side of the nave. What appears here to be a survival of the east range is not the original building. The east side of this structure, however, reveals some clear medieval details. At the ground floor level a fairly large arch of c. 1300 may have contained the window lighting the chapter house. Above this are the blocked remains of a number of lights of apparently fourteenth and fifteenth-century date. These may have lit the dormitory. Close to the Herbert Chapel and on the upper floor level there appears to be a blocked doorway, possibly of much later date.

Completing the group of monastic buildings and still reasonably intact is the great tithe barn marking the west side of the priory precinct.

Further reading
The church guide is by Rev. H.R. Spoule-Jones. (Gloucester, 1977.)

Bardsey
Celtic and, later, Augustinian, Abbey

History
Of all the islands off the Welsh coast none would have aroused the ascetic spirit of the would-be hermit more than Bardsey, known to the Welsh as 'Ynys Enlli'. It would have appeared to a traveller of the Dark Ages as perhaps the most remote and westerly point of the kingdom. Small wonder that it became known as the 'Rome of Wales', on account of the difficulty of reaching it as much as the esteem in which the monastery was held. The monastery was reputedly founded by St Cadfan in the 6th century and became famous through its reputation as the burial place of 20,000 saints. These included Saints Dubricius and Deiniol. Gerald of Wales repeats the ancient claim that old age alone would account for the death of the islanders so that no-one would die before the oldest inhabitant. This peculiarity was allegedly granted through the request of St Lleuddad. Gerald also noted that in his time (late 12th century) the establishment was still Celtic and attached to no particular order. Because there are no remains (apart from an inscribed stone) from the Celtic period some writers have concluded that the monastic institution was at Aberdaron on the mainland and that Bardsey was the site of a hermitage. Considering the fame of the place it seems unlikely that this was the case.

It would appear that about the year 1200 Bardsey became an Augustinian abbey. An agreement with the canons of Aberdaron, dating from 1252, provides direct evidence for this. Bardsey was probably pre-eminent among the group of Augustinian convents in North Wales and held large areas of the Lleyn peninsula. In financial terms, however, it was a poor house, worth only £46 before its dissolution in 1537. It is likely that throughout its history it was exposed to the attentions of marauders of various kinds and never capable of accumulating great wealth.

The buildings

Very little remains of the abbey - so little that the layout of the buildings that comprised the monastery is very much a matter of speculation. Within the modern cemetery there stands a small tower, each side approximately 5.8 m long. It stands to a height of about 7 m but would originally have been more than 11 m high. There is a doorway to the south and indications that walls extended in that direction from the tower. There is also evidence for a wall ex-tending westward from the tower. Suggestions of cloisters and outbuildings seen from the air have yet to be proved on the ground.

Further reading

RCHM Caernarvonshire (West) Item 1518.
"Bardsey - a study in monastic origins". T. Jones in *Transactions of the Caernarvonshire Historical Society* 1983.

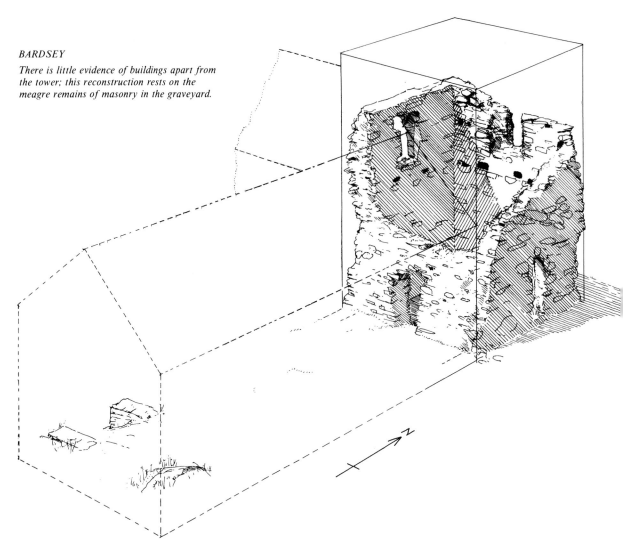

BARDSEY

There is little evidence of buildings apart from the tower; this reconstruction rests on the meagre remains of masonry in the graveyard.

Basingwerk

Cistercian Abbey

History

Basingwerk was one of just two abbeys established in Wales by monks from Savigny in western Normandy. These monks belonged to an order remarkably close to the Cistercians in its reforming character and desire for simplicity. The site of the abbey, founded in 1131 by Ralph II, Earl of Chester, was in a sensitive area bordering on the land of Gwynedd. The Welsh monks of Aberconway, built much later in 1186, seem to have viewed Basingwerk as an outpost of English clerical and political influence and certainly resented its presence. In 1157 the abbot and monks were driven out of the house by the Welsh just ten years after it had become, with the rest of the Savigny abbeys, Cistercian. It then became affiliated to the abbey of Buildwas near Shrewsbury which also had influence with Strata Marcella. This connection did not find favour with the house but was maintained in spite of efforts made to the contrary. 1157 may also mark the date when the monks moved the three miles from the old site to the present one.

In the final Welsh wars the abbey strengthened its English connection and was, not surprisingly, damaged again before a sort of peace settled on the area in 1282. £100 was paid as compensation for war damage by the English crown. There is little record of Basingwerk's later history but in both 1355 and the mid 15th century there is enough to suggest that it was not prosperous. Heavy taxation and perhaps the Black Death had brought the buildings near to total ruin by 1355. The general civil disorder of the 15th century seems to have further involved the abbey. Its income was derived largely from the 1500 acres it owned in Flintshire and also from a valuable property at Glossop in the shadow of the English Pennine Hills.

The latter days of Basingwerk were marked by the abbey's connection with two Welsh poets, Guttain Owain and Tudor Aled, who spent a considerable amount of time there. The last two abbots were father and son - Thomas and Nicholas Pennant - a symbol of the lessening strictness prevailing in the convent.

These two astute men succeeded in converting some of the abbey's wealth into family assets.

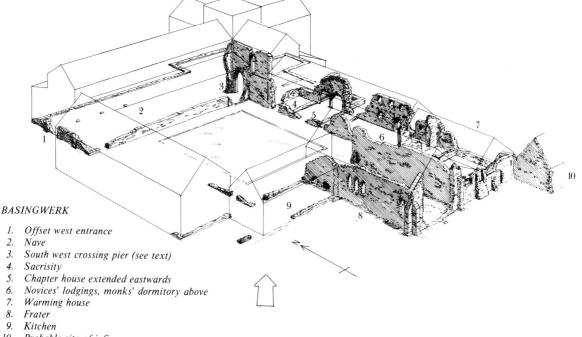

BASINGWERK

1. *Offset west entrance*
2. *Nave*
3. *South west crossing pier (see text)*
4. *Sacristy*
5. *Chapter house extended eastwards*
6. *Novices' lodgings, monks' dormitory above*
7. *Warming house*
8. *Frater*
9. *Kitchen*
10. *Probable site of infirmary*

Early 19th century print of Basingwerk Abbey by Gastineau. The ruins viewed here from the position of the west door into the nave.

At the dissolution of the house in 1535 its annual income was assessed at £163.

The buildings

The two monasteries of the Savignac order in Wales occupied sites rather less obscure and wild than their Cistercian counterparts. Basingwerk stood on level ground close to the estuary of the River Dee, the Clwydian Hills rising gently to the south west.

It appears that in the 12th century the abbey was completed with all the conventual buildings normal to an abbey including a frater along the length of the south range. The church may have been small, perhaps less that 43 m long and much the same size as Aberconway. Early in the 13th century, however, there was substantial building activity. The east range was largely rebuilt and the chapter house extended. The church, whose remains we see now, dates entirely from this period. It was 53 m long and followed the typical Cistercian pattern. It was cruciform, two chapels in each transept, aisles north and south of the nave with a short, aisleless presbytery. Later in the same century the frater was rebuilt on the fashionable north-south axis enabling part of the south range to be used as a kitchen. The large warming house was extended at various stages in the abbey's history, a new fireplace being added in the south wall in the 15th century. It is thought that a substantial infirmary may have existed to the south east under what are now ruined farm buildings.

The present remains of Basingwerk Abbey are fairly extensive though very incomplete. Much of the original appearance can, however, be inferred from the ruins, the details of the south-west crossing pier, for example, reveal the height of the aisle, the line of its roof, the nature of the arches and the space provided for the monks' stalls by recessing the arch. The best remains are in the east range and the frater. The two well-preserved arches in the chapter house mark the thirteenth-century extension of that building, traces of the seating are visible against the walls. Much of the frater is spendidly preserved, particularly the west wall where the reader's pulpit and the serving hatch from the kitchen can be discerned. Another rare survival is the base of the day stairs against the wall of the east range.

Further reading

A.J. Taylor. *Basingwerk Abbey*. Ministry of Public Buildings and Works.

Beddgelert
Augustinian priory

History

Deep in the mountain valleys of Snowdonia, at the foot of Eryri itself, Beddgelert was an ideal spot for a monastic settlement, away from the turmoil of medieval life. Unfortunately, it did not quite succeed in escaping the worst turmoils of the Welsh wars.

Its origins go far back to the 6th century. As a Celtic monastery it was reputed to be one of the oldest in Wales, second only to Bardsey in age. It continued as a Celtic convent at least until the late 12th century when Gerald of Wales mentioned the house. At that time Aberconway Abbey (Cistercian) had obtained enormous tracts of land on the slopes of Eryri within a few yards of Beddgelert Priory itself. The brethren of the priory had long been an integral part of the valley community and resisted, with an appeal to the Pope, what was in effect a takeover bid by the Cistercians. As in modern business, however, it recognised that it could not survive independently and so, shortly, adopted the rule of the new Augustinian order which was proving popular in Gwynedd. From this period

date the oldest parts of the church suggesting that the new connection put fresh life into the priory. The priory was further strengthened by a grant of land by Llywelyn ap Gruffydd in 1268 so that it was in full possession of a large part of the Nant Colwyn valley immediately adjoining the priory buildings.

That was probably the high point of its history. Within a few years it was burnt down, accidentally, during the final Welsh wars. Compensation was paid in 1284 and an appeal made in 1286 succeeded in securing the repair of the buildings. A hundred years later it had again fallen into disrepair and in the early 15th century a fire left it in a desperate condition. The priory was dissolved in 1536 when just three canons served the church and community. One of these was the prior. The annual income was assessed at £69.

The buildings

One would expect the conventual buildings of the Augustinian priory to have been on the south side of the church with, perhaps, a small cloister and adjacent ranges. There is

BEDDGELERT PRIORY

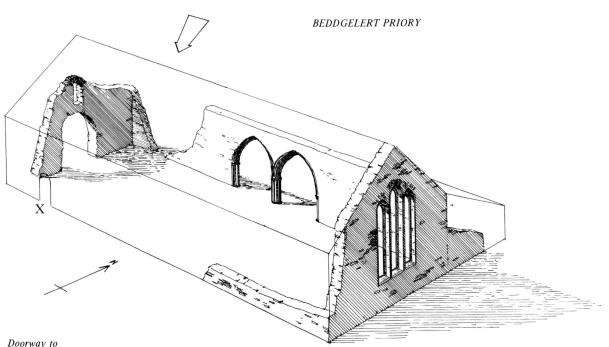

X

Doorway to conventual buildings.

no direct evidence that this was the case but circumstantial evidence supports the proposition. Drawings made at the beginning of the 19th century suggest that buildings abutted the south wall of the church and a door in that wall would have provided access from the conventual buildings to the west end of the nave. This would place the convent to the south west of the church, well away from the river that flows past the east end. Charcoal deposits found south of the church may well be remnants of the destructions of the 13th and 15th centuries. The drawings referred to also suggest that the church consisted of a straightforward nave and chancel with a substantial nave adjoining the length of the north wall. The height of the old windows shown on the south wall indicates that some building may have abutted there, possibly a sheltered cloister walk.

Today there are no remains of the conventual buildings but the church has some notable survivals from the monastic period. Parts of the north wall of the nave may even pre-date the Augustinian church but it is from the period c.1230 that the most distinguished features survive, the period when the church was re-modelled to adapt to the Augustinian order. The fine triple lancets in the chancel east wall are a particular surprise in this rugged part of Snowdonia. The two arches opening from the nave to what is now the north transept are also an unexpected refinement with their deep mouldings. The RCAMW suggests that these may have been meant to run the length of the nave with an extra two arches opening up the north aisle. The north wall of the transept marks the original north wall of the church of which the only remains are in the foundations. The RCAMW also warns us to ignore what appears to be a blocked doorway at the west end of the north wall. This is attributed to the 18th century and not to the medieval period. Most notable of all is the setting of the church amongst the rugged mountains which dominate all around.

Further reading

RCAHM Caernarvonshire (Central) *Transactions of the Caernarvonshire Historical Society*, 1969.

BRECON CATHEDRAL

The Priory Church

1. Almonry
2. Site of west range now built over
3. Cloister entrance to church
4. Site of east range

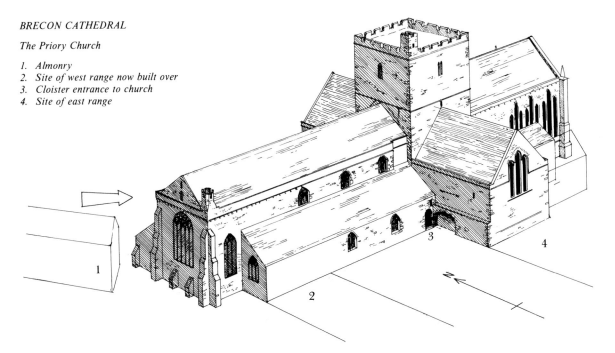

Brecon
Benedictine priory

History

In the surge of Norman conquest in 1093 Brecon was the first victim. In a skirmish on the borders of the town the powerful Welsh leader, Rhys ap Tewdwr, was killed and Bernard Newmarch seized Brecon. Bernard's confessor was a monk of Battle Abbey in Sussex and to that abbey Bernard granted the church of St John the Evangelist in the town. Monks from Battle settled at Brecon but a full conventual settlement may not have been established before 1125. The oldest parts of the church date from this period.

Brecon was an absolute bastion of Norman strength in South Wales. While the Welsh wars raged Brecon Priory grew and the finest parts of the church building were erected during the conflict. Reginald, member of that best known family of marcher lords, de Breos, was buried in the priory. William de Breos, who died in 1211, described Brecon priory as 'this church which I love before all others'. The main fabric of the church owes its existence largely to endowments made by the great marcher families of de Breos, de Bohun and later the Staffords. Within the priory, however, there was some decadence, as Archbishop Pecham found in his visitation of 1283. The prior was accused of drunkenness, embezzling, lying, incontinence and revealing confessions. It is clear that the convent was somewhat demoralised. When Pecham expelled two quasi-members of the convent a local feud broke out involving some unfortunate bloodshed. At this time the priory, with only eight monks and a prior, was below full strength although its value in 1291 of £122 made it one of the wealthier monastic institutions in Wales. Roger, Earl of Hereford, in a charter of c.1150 permitted a minimum convent size of six monks but by 1401 even this number could not be maintained. At the Dissolution in 1534 there were just five monks and a prior. The priory's income was then valued at £112.

The buildings

The priory church of Brecon was among the largest Benedictine. buildings in Wales and survives substantially intact to this day. It appears to have developed from a simple cruciform building without aisles, which was certainly complete by the mid 13th century. By that date, also, chapels extended from the transepts. All this surrounded a massive square tower. Aisles were added to the parochial nave and the chapels in the north transept made into one chapel, the Harvard, in

Brecon Priory.

the 14th century. The essential fabric of the church has not altered since. Remains of the walls of the original nave, before the aisles were constructed, can be seen just to the west of the central crossing.

Of the conventual buildings little, if anything, remains. What appears to be the west range is in fact a subtle addition of the last two centuries incorporating some genuinely original fragments. Evidence within the church indicates that this was indeed the site of the west range. A stairway in the south transept led, presumably, to the dormitory or some part of the east range of which the deanery is a partial survival. The normal cloister arrangements seem to have obtained, with access to the church through a door close to the angle with the south transept. The indications in early prints seem to bear little relation to what may have existed or to what can be seen today but certainly indicate that extensive remains of the priory survived the Dissolution.

The church, now Brecon Cathedral, is one of the most splendid and satisfying in Wales. Of particular quality are the chancel windows (the vaulting is a restoration by Sir Gilbert Scott - 1862). Indications of the monastic period are harder to see but the remains of the night stair are just visible in the corner of the south transept. The day entrance from the cloister into the south aisle is also in good preservation. Approaching the church from the main car park, the almonry, on the right-hand side, clearly preserves features of the medieval period.

Further reading

Powys. In the Buildings of England Series. Penguin.

Brecon Cathedral - the official guide to the Cathedral. A well illustrated general history and description available in the church.

44

Caldey

Priory of the Order of Tiron

History

Caldey is, by tradition, one of the earliest monasteries founded in Wales, reputedly established from Llantwit Major. The Welsh name for the island is Ynys Pyr, supposedly deriving from a founding abbot by the name of Pyro. The history of this Celtic settlement is lost to us but it is reasonable to suppose that the island was exposed to the Norse raids that were the scourge of the Bristol Channel and Welsh coast around the 10th century. The assumption is generally made that by the time of the Norman invasion the monastery was, at best, a shadow of its former self.

In 1113 Henry I granted the island to Robert FitzMartin, founder of St Dogmael's. It is generally thought that Robert's father, Martin of Tiron, was the prime mover in bringing monks from Tiron to St Dogmael's. It is surprising, therefore, to find that Robert passed this gift of Caldey on to his father's widow, Geva. She, in turn, presented the island to St Dogmael's which was well established by 1120. By 1131 a daughter house had been established on the island. Although established for a full convent, Gerald of Wales leads us to believe that by the end of the 12th century there may have been just a solitary monk there. If conditions at the mother house are anything to go by then Caldey did not prosper in later years. By 1535 the annual income was assessed at no more than £5 and only one monk was in residence. The priory was dissolved in 1536.

The buildings

Caldey Priory represents a most important survival from the medieval period in Wales since it seems to preserve something of the spirit of the Celtic era of monasticism. The extant buildings are mostly in a good state of preservation and are of the Tiron period but the tiny size of the priory echoes other island settlements, Burry Holms at Llangennith, St Tudwal's, Bardsey and Ynys Seiriol. It may even be that the buildings we see today represent a reworking of the original conventual layout of the pre-Norman period.

The church consisted of a presbytery with a sanctuary at the east end. At the west end a small tower is surmounted by a crude but picturesque spire. The conventual buildings surrounded a very small (8 m square) cloister

CALDEY PRIORY

1. *Prior's tower*
2. *Gatehouse and guesthouse*
3. *Church*
4. *East range, dormitory on upper floor*

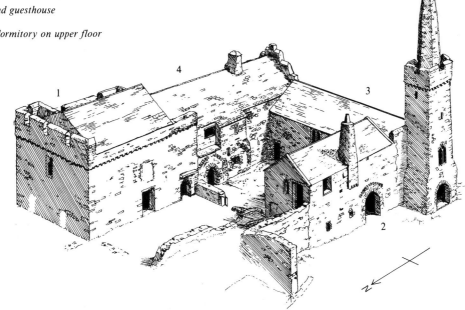

on the north side of the church. The main entrance was directly into this cloister at the south-west corner. The west wing consisted of the gatehouse with a guest room above it. The east wing consisted of the monks' dormitory over a kitchen and warming room. A short passage led directly from the warming room into the refectory which closed the north side of the cloister. The north-east corner of the buildings was occupied by the 'Prior's Tower', a substantial embattled building of which the first floor comprised the prior's lodging.

Apart from the refectory and a small portion of the west wing all these buildings stand today. They make a particularly picturesque grouping whilst the tiny church evokes a special atmosphere with its stone floor and primitive structure. Apart from the church the interiors of the buildings are not open to the public.

Further reading

The Rev. W.D. Bushell. *Caldey: An Island of the Saints*. A thorough monograph available on the island.
See also R. Howells, *Total Community*. Tenby 1975.

Carmarthen

Augustinian priory

History

Carmarthen Priory was, perhaps, the most successful priory in Wales. Its monastic origins probably go back, long before the Norman conquest, to a Celtic 'clas' dedicated to St Teulyddog which may have been founded in the 6th century. If this widely held supposition is true the original church was founded immediately east of the Roman town of Moridunum on the right bank of the River Towy. By 1100 there was already a church within Moridunum - St Peter's - which became the parish church of Carmarthen in later centuries. Henry I apparently granted this and the monastic church to Battle Abbey. Carmarthen thus originated as a Benedictine cell but this status lasted for only a few

years. Bishop Bernard of St David's, finding the cell in poor condition, transferred it to the Augustinian Order of Canons in 1125. The church was dedicated to St John and St Teulyddog. The initial success of the priory may have owed something to this acceptance of its Welsh origins and the fact that Welshmen were common as members of the convent. Another factor was the income it derived from its possessions in the old town of Carmarthen (Moridunum) whilst the new walled town grew round the castle. An early endowment was the church of St Peter's in the old town.

The valuation of 1291 does not seem to reflect the true financial strength of the priory, the figure given being just under £30. At that time, apart from the old town of Carmarthen, it possessed some 1500 acres of ploughlands. During the next century several churches were appropriated to the priory, burgages were gained and the house became wealthier. Its income was assessed in 1336 as £66. In spite of the Black Death and the impoverishment that seemed to afflict all Welsh houses at the time it was still occupied by six canons in 1379. By the end of the 14th century the priory held 22 churches and chapels and its income must have been about £200.

A temporary check to the growth of the priory came in the Glyndwr rebellion when the house was sacked and seriously damaged. How long the recovery took is difficult to tell but by the 16th century it appears to have been in a healthy condition. The provision of hospitality to travellers, particularly wealthy ones, was always a serious drain on the finances of a convent and the provision of alms to the poor often, by necessity, neglected. But Carmarthen was able to meet all these obligations generously. Immediately before the Dissolution in 1536 it was said to be occupied by a prior and eight canons with 80 people functioning around the buildings and alms provided for some 80 poor people. At the Dissolution Carmarthen Priory was assessed at £164.

The buildings

This important priory has, unfortunately, suffered complete destruction, notably at the hands of Lord Cawdor in the 18th century, who required the site for lead works. Excavations

Detail of Buck's engraving of Carmarthen.
The figure 7 marks the remaining monastic building.

position of some of the buildings but their full extent and purpose remain very much a matter of conjecture. The church appears to have been large, at least 55 m long and probably much longer after an extension to its east end. Excavations indicate a cruciform church with a lengthy south chapel or, possibly, a chapter house. There is good evidence for an east range extending from the south transept. It was still standing in the last century and was known as 'The Prior's House'. All these lay within an extensive enclosure with a gateway to the north west. The gateway survives although its details are concealed within a terrace at the bottom of Old Priory Road. The church and conventual buildings occupied the south-east half of the precinct closely overlooking the River Towy.

carried out in 1979 by the Dyfed Archaeological Trust together with information from nineteenth-century maps have established the

Further reading

Alcwyn C. Evans. St John's Priory, Carmarthen. *Arch. Camb.* 1876.

Terrence James. Excavations at the Augustinian Priory of St John and St Teulyddog, Carmarthen, 1979. *Arch. Camb.* 1985.

Chepstow Priory — the Norman west door.

47

Chepstow
Benedictine priory

History

Chepstow was the first monastery founded in Wales by the Normans who established that classic combination during the invasion - church and castle. In the shadow of the mighty fortress of Chepstow Castle, William FitzOsbern founded the priory of St Mary. He was one of the most powerful men in these islands apart from King William himself whose close friend and ally he was. FitzOsbern was Seneschal of Normandy and Earl of Hereford and had previously founded an abbey at Cormeilles near Lisieux. To this abbey he gave the priory of Chepstow, known as Striguil in those days. It was thus established as an alien priory, a point of weakness in future years. Without the foreign connection the priory might have been expected to prosper in later years.

The priory never grew to any great size and there is no record of there ever being more than four monks and a prior there (1370) although it may have begun with a full convent of twelve monks. One of its important functions was to serve the chapel in the castle where a monk was expected to say mass three times a week. The military connection, together with the fact that the monks, this being an alien priory, were normally French, indicates why the Benedictine Order never gained popularity in Wales.

In 1291 the priory was valued at a little under £35 and owned 300 acres with 40 sheep and seven cows. Although modest in wealth it already supported an impressive priory church. Following the normal Benedictine arrangement, the choir and transepts belonged to the monks but the nave was for parish use and served by a vicar who had a room in the priory.

In 1294 came the first of the Crown seizures that was to afflict all alien priories. For

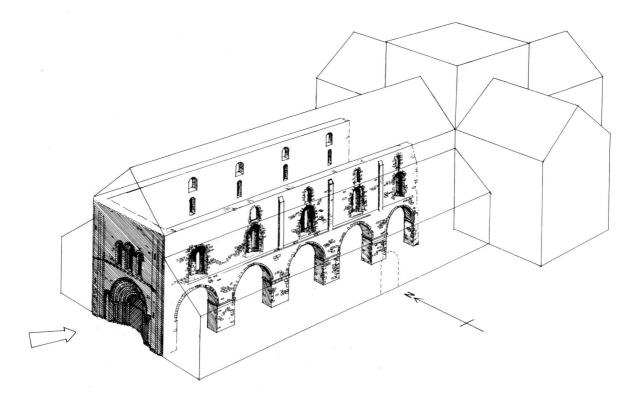

Chepstow Priory — reconstruction.

48

Margam Abbey – The Chapter House – architectural highlight of the ruins.

Talley Abbey – Crossing tower.

The Frater – Basingwerk Abbey.

more than a hundred years Chepstow was to suffer as a result. During the period 1394-8 we know that there were no monks in the convent. The monks of alien priories close to the sea were often required to withdraw altogether from their houses. Although there was an improvement after 1399 the final seizure took place in 1414. Chepstow was, at first, attached to Bermondsey and there were later plans to grant it to God's House College, Cambridge. By 1442, however, the priory became independent, served by English monks. This does not seem to have improved the fortunes of the house and by 1534 only a prior and one monk were present. The annual income was assessed at £32. It was dissolved in 1536.

The buildings

Sadly, the Dissolution saw the prompt destruction of the monastery by the townsfolk. The monks' choir and transepts, together with the conventual buildings, were destroyed. It is highly likely that, considering the persistent poverty of the house, the monastic buildings were already in a dilapidated condition. The nave was now walled off so that it could continue to be used. Some inferences can, however, be drawn from the remaining nave which survives in large part to this day. The church was cruciform and large, almost the proportions of a small cathedral and certainly comparable to Brecon. The interior of a small English cathedral such as, say, Chichester, would give a fair impression of the appearance of the priory church of Chepstow - massive rectangular Norman piers of six bays, flanked by side aisles. The sixth bay is inferred from the position of the crossing pier, the base of which has been preserved. This same pier implies the transepts of the original church, as well as the tower which fell c.1700. A print in Cox's *Monmouthshire* indicates some of the survivals of the old church before the side aisles were demolished and the nave arches blocked in. The present additions to the original Norman nave date from 1891 but restore something of the spaciousness which was a quality of the monastic church. The west tower was built in 1706 after the collapse of the central tower but the west doorway is a splendid survival from the Norman period.

Of the conventual buildings nothing is known except that excavations have indicated that they were of irregular alignment.

Further reading

John P. Harris, *The Priory and Parish Church of St Mary, Chepstow*. A fairly comprehensive church guide.

Conway I
Cistercian abbey

History

In 1186 a group of monks left Strata Florida to establish a Cistercian house in North Wales. What encouragement they were given, and by whom, in the form of early endowments, we do not know. Their first settlement was at Rhedynog Felen close to the present-day town of Caernarvon. Some four or five years later the convent moved to Conway and there established an abbey that was to be of great importance during the following century. Unusually, for a Cistercian house, it was not far distant from an existing power centre, in this case of the North Wales princes at Deganwy. This proximity may well have contributed to the importance attached to the house by the last Welsh rulers. In 1199 Llywelyn ap Iorwerth made enormous grants of land to the abbey including much of central Snowdonia, and he became recognised as the founder of the abbey which went on to possess a greater acreage of land than any other Welsh monastery. It was certainly the most significant house in North Wales. In spite of, or maybe because of this, the English restricted the power of the abbey in church affairs and would not admit the sub-prior, Rotoland, to be Bishop of Bangor (c.1200) even though he had been unanimously elected to that position by the local community.

The early days of the abbey were marked by poor relations with neighbouring houses, particularly Beddgelert which it hoped to absorb into its enormous properties. Also, in 1202, the abbot was reported to General Chapter for rarely celebrating the mass. Llywelyn the Great, however, held the abbey in high esteem and was buried there in 1240.

In the final years of Welsh independence the abbot of Aberconway became an important negotiator between Llywelyn the Last and the English king. In 1262 he was the sole representative of Llywelyn in negotiations.

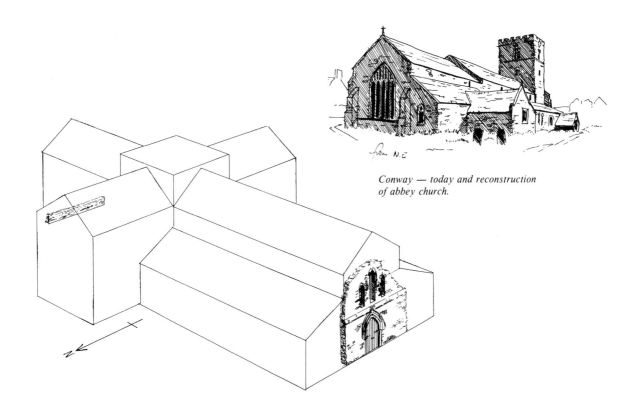

Conway — today and reconstruction of abbey church.

When, some twenty years later, the Welsh were finally crushed, Edward I treated the abbey generously. Not only could he see that it was bad policy to alienate such an influential house but he also had plans to establish a town and castle on the strategic site held by the abbey. This required the moving of the convent to a new site, a second Conway, and for that it was more expedient to co-operate than coerce.

The buildings

Immediately the monks had vacated their monastery in 1294 the abbey church was adapted to the needs of the growing town and its inhabitants. That adaptation has been a continuing process ever since, which has made it a matter of surmise as to the shape of the original Cistercian church. Some authorities have taken the view that the church, like Cymer, was never completed beyond the construction of the nave, but more recently the view has been taken that a simple, cruciform church was completed. Such a church would have had aisles to the north and south, short transepts and a small choir with a total length of the order of 45 m. In most respects, therefore, Basingwerk would present a fair model for Conway's abbey church. Substantial parts of the west end of the church survive, notably a fine triple lancet of the early 13th century above a door of comparable date. The east extremity of the present church, in its lower courses, is also of the monastic period, thus delineating the length of the original church. The south doorway also uses some material from the abbey church.

There is considerable evidence that the conventual buildings existed to the north and east of the church but their layout is not known. Models proposed for this layout suggest that it was rather unorthodox.

Further reading

L.A.S. Butler, An excavation in the vicarage garden, Conway 1961. *Arch Camb.* 1964.
R.W. Hays, *The History of the Abbey of Aberconway.* Cardiff 1963.

Conway II
Rebuilt Cistercian abbey of Aberconway

History
The monks of Aberconway, after less than a century in their abbey, had no choice but to accede to Edward I's request that they move. But Edward was sensitive to the feelings of this representative institution of a conquered people and provided the means for them to build a splendid new abbey a few miles up the Conway valley. By 1284 the monks were able to move to Maenan, the new site, and every financial assistance was made to ensure that the move was not distressing. In 1291 the abbey was valued at £76 and is recorded as having 560 sheep on its many acres (this seems to be a very modest piece of accounting).

In the post-war period, however, the abbey seems to have fallen on hard times like many other houses in Wales. The Glyndwr rebellion was not supported by the abbey until its last three years. This reluctance may have been connected to the original indebtedness of the abbey to Edward I. The worst episodes in the abbey's history came, however, in the 15th century. The abbot, John ap Rhys, apparently conducted a feud with Strata Florida and took this to extremes when he led some of his monks and some soldiers on a raid of that abbey. He imprisoned the convent, stopped services and took animals and valuables.

It seems very likely that the abbey was itself despoiled in 1468 when the Yorkist army passed through the Conway valley in the Wars of the Roses. There is some slight evidence, also, of moral laxity in the abbey in the latter part of the century. The fabric of the buildings was also in poor condition since, in 1489, the abbot, Dafydd ap Owain, felt it necessary to carry out rebuilding and restoration. Although valued at £162 in 1535, Conway could not have been in sound financial order at its suppression in 1537. The destruction of its buildings was especially thorough whilst, ironically, the original Welsh church in Conway town survives in part to this day.

The buildings
Our knowledge of the buildings at Maenan rests entirely on the work of archaeologists, particularly those excavations carried out in 1968 by Butler and Evans. If the interpretation of the scant remains discovered is correct then the second Conway was built along the lines established by the South Wales monasteries of Neath and Margam which were extensively remodelled at about the same time. The church would have been about 68 m long and the nave 16 m wide. This large church had aisles continued by an ambulatory round the choir.

Of the conventual buildings there are no remains but they are thought to have existed to the east of the church. There remains nothing to be seen of the abbey. The site is owned by the Maenan Abbey Hotel on the east edge of the Conway valley a little to the north of Llanrwst.

Further reading
L.A.S. Butler and D.H. Evans. The Cistercian Abbey of Aberconway at Maenan, Gwynedd. Excavations in 1968. *Arch. Camb.* 1980.

Cwmhir
Cistercian abbey

History
Few places in Wales speak more eloquently than Cwmhir of Welsh aspirations for nationhood dashed by centuries of defeat and poverty. The abbey was founded originally by an indigenous Welsh ruler. Maelienydd was a small state in mid Wales frequently under control of the marcher lords, particularly the Mortimers. Maredudd, son of Madog ap Idnerth, briefly held Maelienydd during a respite from Norman domination and in 1143 he approached Whitland to establish a Cistercian abbey deep in the hills of his ancestral homeland. This foundation was probably at Tyfaenor, about a mile below the present site of Cwmhir. Plans for the abbey were apparently aborted when Maredudd was killed in 1146 and the Normans regained control of Maelienydd.

In 1176, with Lord Rhys dominant in South Wales, conditions were more propitious for a Welsh house of monks in the area. Maredudd's son, Cadwallon, refounded Cwmhir on the present site. He and his brother, Einion Clud, became the chief benefactors of Cwmhir Abbey. Although by the end of the century the Mortimers were once again in control of the area the position of the abbey was regularised when Roger Mortimer recognised and increased the abbey's holdings. The abbey's fortunes over the next hundred years or so were mixed. That some members of the convent were deeply involved in secular affairs is demonstrated by the monk who deliberately led Henry III's army into an ambush near Hay in 1231 thus bringing down considerable destruction on one of Cwmhir's granges and, possibly, on the abbey itself.

It was about this time that the abbey church was rebuilt. The new church was planned on a scale unequalled in Wales and with few parallels elsewhere in Britain. The suggestion has been made (C. A. Ralegh Radford) that the ambitious plan for the abbey reflected an attempt by the northern princes of Wales to create a religious and political centre for the country, uniting north and south in mid Wales. The nave alone, 74 m in length, would have reflected the upsurge in national hopes and pride. It may have been the destruction of 1231 or the ensuing poverty that made it impossible to finish the building but only the nave was completed. Although a convent of more than 50 monks may have been planned the abbey could never have supported so many. In the taxation of 1291 Cwmhir was valued at only £35 although owning over 3000 acres of sheep runs and pasture (but only 300 sheep). With the defeat of Llywelyn the Last a few miles away, not only the hopes of Welsh independence died but also hopes of completing Cwmhir Abbey. Had it been completed it would undoubtedly have been one of the wonders of ecclesiastical architecture in the country. Llywelyn was buried in the abbey but his grave is not marked.

In the Glyndwr rebellion the abbey was 'spoilid and defacid' (Leland) and may not have been restored extensively. At the Dissolution in 1536 there were just three monks and the annual income of the house was assessed at only £25.

South wall of nave — Cwmhir Abbey.

The buildings

Leland's description of the buildings shortly after the Dissolution is significant. He describes them as standing

> betwixt 2 great hilles in Melennith ... no chirch in Wales is seen of such length as the fundation of walles there begon doth show; but the third part of this worke was never finished. Al the house was spoilid and defacid by Owen Glindour.

The abbey was clearly in a poor condition then and rapidly deteriorated. The arcade at Llanidloes church, a particularly beautiful example of thirteenth-century work, survives from the abbey and shows us what magnificence may have existed at Cwmhir. The nave of the church was 75 m long with 14 arches in each arcade, aisles north and south of the nave. There was no west door and the main entrance was in the south wall near the west end. Another, smaller door gave access from the cloister close to the intended transepts. The church was never completed beyond the west wall of the transepts.

The principal investigations of the site were those carried out by T. Wilson (1824) and S.W. Williams (account published in *Arch.*

Camb. 1895). Excavations in 1824 revealed substantial remains of the conventual buildings to the south east, particularly the refectory and kitchen areas. A tentative plan drawn by Williams in 1894 shows the site of the east and west ranges. The east range, in particular, is discordant with a normal monastic layout and probably fitted more normally with the original church before the ambitious rebuilding occurred.

Cwmhir today is, in many ways, a disappointing site since the remains are not impressive. Considering the destruction suffered by the buildings before and after the Dissolution it is pleasing, however, to find a considerable length of the nave's south wall standing with a few mouldings visible. The basic outline of the church is easily apparent and the site, by the Clywedog stream, quite beautiful. The finest remains are, however, in Llanidloes church where the six bay arcade is still worth seeing. There is little doubt that the arcade was transferred there almost immediately after the Dissolution and was incorporated in a substantial rebuilding of the town church.

Further reading

C.A. Ralegh Radford, The Cistercian Abbey of Cwmhir, Radnorshire. *Arch. Camb* 1982.

Cymer
Cistercian abbey

History

Cymer was one of the last Cistercian foundations in Wales and has much in common with other such abbeys, not least that the church was never completed. In 1198 monks from the abbey at Cwmhir in the hills of mid Wales came to Cymer under the patronage of the cousin of Llywelyn the Great - Maredudd ap Cynan. Llywelyn himself made gifts to the new foundation which was built close to the tidal limit of the Mawddach estuary, deep amongst the mountains of Merioneth. Although endowed with large tracts of mountainous waste it was not noted for its sheep, as were many similar abbeys, but for its fishing and shipping. Together with dairying and mining

they were significant features of the abbey's economy. It was very much a Welsh house and suffered as a result of the Welsh wars. In 1241 the monks were ordered to disperse by the General Chapter, presumably a reflection of the troubled times. Llywelyn ap Gruffydd (the Last) used the abbot on occasions for political negotiations, just as he used the abbot of Aberconway. After the wars, however, Cymer was not favoured as was Aberconway and received only £80 compensation for damages.

The nave of the church and the conventual buildings were completed during the first 100 years of the abbey's life. The loss of Welsh independence and the ensuing poverty seem to have dampened the hopes and ambitions of the monks and, save for a little tower built at the west end of the nave, no further building took place. The church remained without transepts or what might be recognised as a presbytery. Edward I visited the abbey frequently between 1283 and 1295 and even gave £5 towards the building work.

In 1351 the abbot was given the dubious privilege of collecting the Crown taxes in North Wales, a responsibility that must have been uncomfortable for such a Welsh house. Valued at under £12 in 1291, it was never wealthy. By 1400 there were probably no more that five monks in the convent. In 1441 the presiding abbot was the notorious John ap Rhys from Conway (*q.v.*) whose deliberate mismanagement impoverished the abbey even further. It would appear that he was ousted by 1443 but the disturbances which continued to afflict the house may have been due to his activities.

Political troubles in Wales a decade later caused the abbey to be taken into royal custody. The economy of the house continued to decline, the convent was in disarray and, once again, the question of its dispersal was raised. From then on the abbacy seems to have been regarded as something of a sinecure since English monks with matters of greater import on their hands held the post on at least two occasions. The closing days of Cymer's life brought no better days and in the 1520s it was probably once again the victim of mismanagement.

Cymer was one of the last Welsh houses to be suppressed, due in part to its remoteness. The suppression took place in March 1537, the house having been valued at £51, the poorest in North Wales.

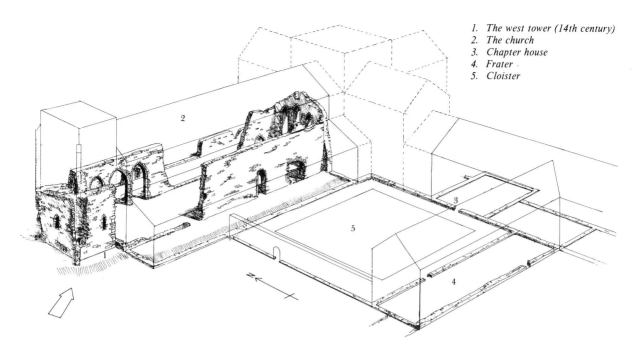

1. *The west tower (14th century)*
2. *The church*
3. *Chapter house*
4. *Frater*
5. *Cloister*

Cymer Abbey. The broken lines indicate the intended layout of the church, the east end and the sacrisity were never completed.

The buildings

The church at Cymer Abbey was never completed and the whole complex of buildings covered only a small area. The plan of the buildings was clearly meant to be conventional in layout, a cruciform, aisled church with the eastern range of the conventual buildings extending from the south transept. The cloister and the western range would have adjoined the nave in the normal way. But the transepts and choir were never built and fairly early in the 14th century plans for their construction must have been abandoned. This left the thirteenth-century nave with aisles, north and south, terminated at the eastern end by a fine triple lancet window. As an afterthought, in the 14th century, a small tower of unknown height was erected at the western end of the nave. The eastern range of the conventual buildings was built with the clear expectation, on the other hand, that the transepts would be built. A small chapter house in the eastern range would have been beneath the monks' dormitory. The south range was entirely taken up with a frater which had an east-west axis in the old style of Cistercian layouts. There is no evidence of a western range abutting the cloister but the adjoining farmhouse, west of the church, probably marks the site of and incorporates some fabric from the guest-house.

The remains are in the care of Cadw and are very few apart from the church itself. The walls of that building survive to the height at which the aisle roof would have abutted the main wall of the church. The blocking wall at the east end is largely intact with the triple lancet windows in a good state of preservation. In the south wall of the nave the liturgical arrangements of the sedilia and piscina with Celtic ornamentation should be noted. The aisles were separated from the nave for most of their length by walls, but a three bay arcade provided an opening towards the west end. The north arcade survives intact. The monks' stalls probably extended as far as this arcade. The small west tower can be seen, in part, adjoining the arcade.

Only the foundations of the conventual buildings can be seen. The deep ditch that runs through the frater block marks the drain that served the reredorter and, probably, the kitchen.

Further reading

David H. Williams, The Cistercians in West Wales. I. Cymer Abbey. *Arch. Camb.* 1981.

Ewenny

Benedictine priory

History

The evidence of pre-Norman memorial stones on the site of Ewenny Priory strongly suggests that there was a Welsh church here well before the Normans arrived. During the occupation of Glamorgan in Norman times William de Londres settled in the area, his local focus of strength being Ogmore Castle. Rather than establishing, as was common practice, a monastic convent in the shadow of the castle he gave the nearby church of St Michael to Gloucester Abbey and in 1141, when William's son Maurice made provision, a monastery was established for a prior and 12 monks. The fortunes of the house continued to be closely linked to the de Londres family and Ogmore Castle. Maurice's son, William, was the most significant contributor to the buildings as we see them today but the original nave of the secular church was erected by the first

William. Gerald of Wales referred to the 'little cell' of Ewenny and by 1291 it was valued at only £56. When the de Londres family died out in the following century the priory could look forward to a very modest future and no more building took place. As a result of this impoverishment we now have the priceless treasure of an unaltered Benedictine priory church with very little diminution of its original plan.

At the time of the Dissolution of 1535 the priory was valued at £59 with only a prior and two monks in residence.

The buildings

The priory church was added to the existing church of St Michael in such a way that a typical cruciform shape was assumed. Chapels were built on to both transepts which, together with the eastern limb of the church, was for the monks' use alone. At the same time the conventual buildings would have been

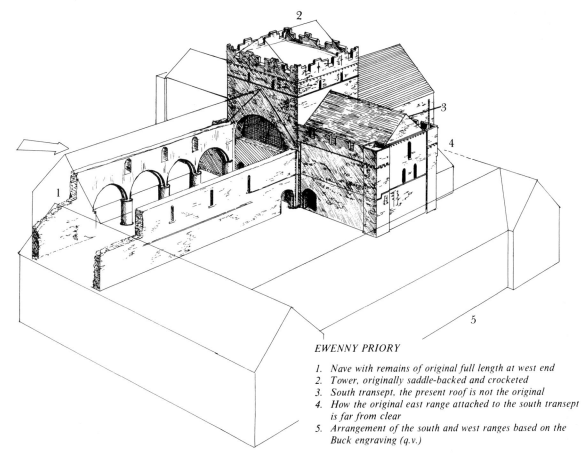

EWENNY PRIORY

1. *Nave with remains of original full length at west end*
2. *Tower, originally saddle-backed and crocketed*
3. *South transept, the present roof is not the original*
4. *How the original east range attached to the south transept is far from clear*
5. *Arrangement of the south and west ranges based on the Buck engraving (q.v.)*

erected and a wall of strong military appearance surrounded the monastery. This would have offered some form of protection to the convent which was relatively far from the shelter of the nearest castle. The walls, which had towers and gatehouses north and south, were of dubious effectiveness and appear to have been incomplete.

When the priory was established various changes were made to the church apart from the addition of the monastic portions. The height of the nave was raised, the tower was built and a north aisle was added to accommodate more people. The only indication left of this aisle is in the sturdy arcade separating the present north aisle from the nave. The stone screen between the nave and the presbytery today gives some indication of the ways in which the monastic and secular functions of the church were separated.

Access to the conventual buildings was gained through the door at the south east end of the nave and by the night stairs. These latter consisted of a spiral in the thickness of the wall of the south transept, rather like Brecon Priory. The east range that the stairs led to is no longer visible and the horizontal sill that runs along the outside south wall of the south transept makes it difficult to speculate as to its possible appearance. The cloister clearly occupied the normal area and there is enough material in the present building to indicate a substantial west range. The south range is, at best, inferred from this but the Buck engraving of 1741 gives a fair indication of what the arrangements were like on this side. About 1800 the conventual buildings were pretty thoroughly dismantled but some remains were incorporated into the building on the present site of the west range.

There is free access to Ewenny Church and the monastic portion is in the care of Cadw. Although the north transept and all the chapels are gone their remains are sufficient to imagine something of their appearance. Splendid examples of Norman architecture abound throughout the building but the nave has been shortened. The north aisle, which collapsed in 1803, is a rebuilding. The building on the site of the west range is private but can be viewed through the north gateway of the walls which remain in a good state of preservation.

Goldcliff
Benedictine priory

History
It is especially sad that there are no physical remains of the buildings of such a notable priory as Goldcliff. In medieval times it was a significant port near the mouth of the River Usk. Trade was carried on with the other side of the Bristol Channel and this is reflected in the endowments of the priory. Robert de Chandos, the local Norman magnate, came from the area of Bec in France. Henry I persuaded him to give the church at Goldcliff to the abbey at Bec (c.1113). De Chandos himself was buried in the church having generously endowed the priory in previous years. Although in Wales, Goldcliff had considerable possessions in Somerset across the Channel. This stored up difficulties for the future, a French priory sited in Wales but with English lands as a principal endowment.

Initially it was intended that a full convent of a prior and twelve monks should be at Goldcliff and in the early years there is nothing to suggest that this was not the case. The priory appears to have thrived. In 1291 it would seem that it was the wealthiest Benedictine house in Wales. It was valued at £171, owned some 1300 acres of land and is known to have had a convent of 25 monks at about this time. But decline had already set in a few years earlier. Bad relations existed with the patron of the time, Gilbert de Clare, Earl of Gloucester. In 1290 Edward I noted the difficulties of the house and made various concessions to ease its problems. By 1297 the convent had been quickly reduced to 15 and the priory was deprived of much of its natural income. Thereafter decline was rapid and greatly exacerbated by the alien status of the priory after 1295. Over the next century the priory was taken into Crown hands on four occasions for lengthy periods.

As if the French wars were not a sufficient trial to the priory it now came into conflict with its current patron, Philip de Columbers. As a result of the dispute between him and the prior, Ralph de Runceville, the Somerset and Devon holdings of the house were considerably despoiled. In 1318 Ralph, proven to be a descendant of the earlier patron de Chandos, was removed from office but appears to have avenged himself by removing many valuables from the place and leaving it with substantial debts to its patron. Prior William de St Albino, who replaced Ralph, had a most uncomfortable time in the following years. At one stage, he found himself imprisoned in Usk Castle, his freedom depending on a payment of 100 marks. Again, the priory's property and possessions at various Welsh granges were taken from it. At the same time even nature conspired against the house when it was largely inundated by the encroaching sea.

It seems a long catalogue of ills besetting this priory and much to its credit that it maintained its convent. Once again it was afflicted in 1322 when a monk of nearby Tintern Abbey, by dint of a forged papal bull, insinuated himself into the position of prior of Goldcliff. His personal patron was Sir John Inge of Somerset who, for nominal annual payments, took possession of many of Goldcliff's properties in Somerset and Devon. Thus deprived of income due from valuable manors the priory reached the nadir of its fortunes. Although the fraud was uncovered within a year the damage was lasting. For the next few decades, however, the priory was spared the deprivations caused by nature and by mismanagement but not the difficulties caused by its status as an alien priory.

In 1410 additional monks from Bec arrived to help maintain the strength of the priory. The sea continued to encroach and, in 1424, destroyed half of the church which served both parish and priory. The last tribulation for Goldcliff came just before its dissolution. Around 1439 Lawrence de Bonneville was prior but recalled to Bec on a suggestion of mismanagement. A monk from Gloucester took his place and in 1441 the priory was annexed by Tewkesbury Abbey. This annexation was, according to the testimony of de Bonneville, a tempestuous and violent affair. De Bonneville had refused to return to Bec and now found himself imprisoned at Usk and Abergavenny Castles. The priory was broken into and the eight monks of the convent expelled. Tewkesbury's hold on the priory was not final, however, and it was granted, ultimately, to Eton in 1467. By that time all monsastic activity had finished.

The buildings
Williams (*op. cit.*) notes a cellar in the present farmhouse but nothing is readily visible to the casual visitor. The site on top of the 'Gold Cliff' is impressive and the wide views across the Severn Estuary remind one of the English connections of this house.

Further reading
David H. Williams, Goldcliff Priory. In the *Monmouthshire Antiquary* (Vol 3). One of a series of outstanding monographs on individual monasteries in Wales and a definitive account of Goldcliff Priory.

Grace Dieu
Cistercian abbey

No monastery in Wales had a more painful or protracted birth than the little abbey of Grace Dieu near Monmouth. It was established at the request of John, Lord of Monmouth and through the agency of the abbey of Morimund in France. Dore Abbey, a few miles upstream from Monmouth on the Monnow, being a daughter house to Morimund, acted as 'midwife' in the birth of Grace Dieu which was established in 1226. The exact site of this first abbey is not known, it may have been close to the later site but conclusive evidence is wanting.

Because it was established through English agencies of the Cistercian order it was not viewed favourably by the Welsh who apparently felt that the land it was built on was rightly theirs. In 1233, during a raid of Llywelyn the Great, the abbey was completely destroyed. A new site was sought by John of Monmouth and by 1236 the monks were establishing themselves by the Trothy stream some 6 km west of Monmouth. The abbey may have been assisted by compensation paid by Llywelyn in 1236. The abbey seemed set fair for the next few years but the Welsh wars of the 13th century appear to have been the cause of further ruination sometime before 1276. It may be that yet another change of site took place but if so it would have been very close to the second abbey.

As can be imagined, such traumatic events left Grace Dieu impoverished. In the 1291 assessment it was valued at only £18 (nearby Tintern £145) although endowed with 1800 acres around the Trothy and Monnow valleys and the Forest of Dean. Monks were involved in farming (14 cows and 22 sheep), wool production and iron ore smelting. In spite of this the abbey's poverty was considerable and the abbot of 1335 was excommunicated for failure to pay his tithe. It was, of course, a difficult time for all Welsh monasteries, but Grace Dieu was the least well equipped to face such exigencies. It may be that it already failed to maintain anything like the full convent of 12 monks and an abbot; at the Dissolution in 1536 there were just two monks.

The abbey appears to have been free of the corruptions that besmirch the annals of so many monasteries but may well have been a victim of Sir John Inges's commercial adventurism (see Goldcliff) when it forfeited its rights to him at one of its granges in 1337. In the next century it was also troubled by the maladministration of its abbot, Richard Moyne. At the time of the Dissolution Grace Dieu, at £19, was valued as the poorest Cistercian house in all England and Wales. After a stormy first 50 years it would appear to have led the quietest and poorest life imaginable, hidden away in a wood and probably unnoticed by any but those involved in its life.

No remains are to be seen, in fact the precise location of the abbey is still open to some speculation. The site is visible, a meadow by the Trothy stream west of Monmouth now astride the Offa's Dyke path. Excavations carried out in 1970 and 1971 by D.H. Williams probably touched the northern fringes of the abbey buildings (see *Monmouthshire Antiquary* 3).

Further reading

D.H. Williams, Grace Dieu Abbey. *The Monmouthshire Antiquary* Volume 1 Part 4 1964.

Haverfordwest
Augustinian priory of St Mary and St Thomas

History

Haverfordwest appears to have had a quiet history, never growing to great size or influence. Interestingly, much of the ground plan survives although most of the ruins are negligible.

The date of the foundation is not known but was probably about 1180. The founder was Robert FitzRichard and it has been suggested that the foundation may have been connected with Caradog, a Welsh monk whose activities were contemporaneous with the Norman conquest of Wales. Robert's grandfather persecuted Caradog but Robert's father patronised the Celtic monk. The centre of much of Caradog's activities, nearby St Ishmaels, became one of the churches under the priory. The house was established for 13 canons of the Augustinian Order just half a mile south of the town of Haverfordwest which had been established by Gilbert de Clare some 70 years before. The Augustinian Order would have been more acceptable to any Welsh connections the house might have had rather than the dishonoured Benedictine monks as typified by nearby Pembroke.

Little is known of the history of Haverfordwest Priory but in 1284, at the end of the Welsh wars, it appears to have displeased Pecham in his tour of the houses of South Wales. He found the finances badly managed and had to appoint two trusty canons as treasurers. Clearly the discipline of the convent was a little lax. The canons were enjoined to take their meals in the frater according to rules of the Order. The prior was required not to separate himself from the canons at meal times unless some pressing occasion demanded. Pecham also sought, among other things, that left-over food should be used for distribution to the poor. Compared with houses such as Brecon, however, these rebukes seem mild indeed and this 'rap on the knuckles' may had been a stimulant to keep the convent vigilant in observing the rules of the Order.

Although valued in 1291 at only £17 the priory had six local churches appropriated to it. At its suppression in 1536 it was valued at £135 with a prior, two canons and four priests in residence.

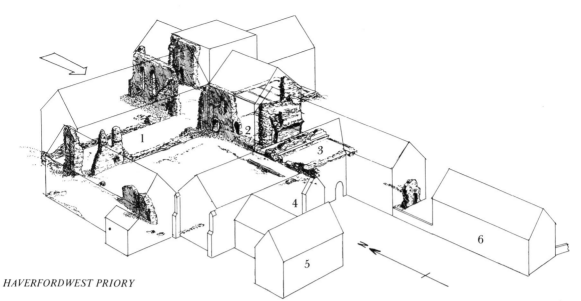

HAVERFORDWEST PRIORY

Reconstruction of Haverfordwest Priory.

1. Cruciform Church
2. East Range, dormitory above, chapter house below
3. South Range – frater
4. Kitchen and buttery
5. West Range. Cellarer's buildings
6. Probable position of infirmary

Remains of the Priory — Haverfordwest, early 19th century.

The buildings

Thanks to excavation carried out between 1922 and 1924 by A.W. Clapham, R.E.M. Wheeler and E.A.R. Rahbula, we now have a fairly complete idea of the extent and nature of the priory at Haverfordwest. The church, dating from the 13th century, was of a simple cruciform shape without side aisles. There are, however, traces of a north aisle added in the last decades of the priory's life. The overall length of the church was some 46 m. The choir was separated from the nave by a stone pulpitum (screen) with a doorway in the middle. The layout of the conventual buildings was entirely conventional. The east range had a small rectangular chapter house of the 13th century beneath the canons' dormitory, the latter can be inferred from the night stairs let into the west wall of the south transept. The frater occupied the entire length of the south range with cooking arrangements adjoining the south wall. An extension of the east range has been interpreted as the infirmary whilst the four rooms of the west range comprised the normal cellars and store rooms. This range is possibly of a slightly later date than the others. The principal remains are of the church. The south east corner of the nave stands and parts of the north and south transepts, all with thirteenth-century lights. In the south transept can be seen the night stairs in the width of the west wall. This site, now in the hands of Cadw, is currently being improved so that details of the ranges can be seen more clearly. The various ranges can be easily discerned and some details of the cloister area are now apparent.

Further reading

E.A.R. Rahbula, Further Excavations at Haverfordwest Priory. *Arch. Camb.* 1924.

Llanllugan
Cistercian house of nuns

History

Llanllugan lies in the heart of the ancient realm of Powys, now remote in the rolling hills north of Newtown. It was founded, pro- bably about 1200, by the Lord of Cydewain - Maredudd ap Rhotpert, and came under the control of Strata Marcella. It

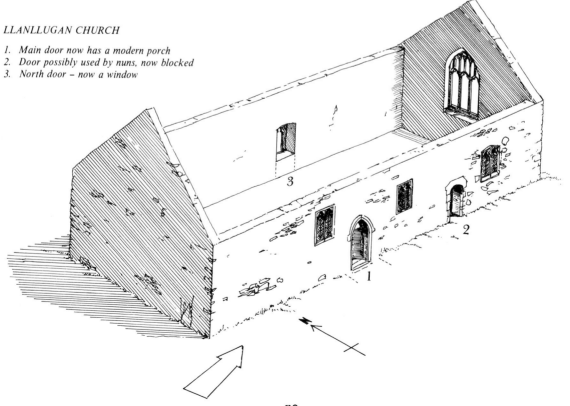

LLANLLUGAN CHURCH

1. *Main door now has a modern porch*
2. *Door possibly used by nuns, now blocked*
3. *North door – now a window*

may have been regarded as a refounding of the first house of nuns established from Strata Marcella - the disastrous Llansantfraed in Elfael. It is possible that there had been a Celtic church on the site but there is no indication of it in the founding charter. As Leland said of it more than 300 years later, it was a 'veri poore nunneri', not well endowed and with just two and a half carucates of land together with some revenues from two local churches making an annual income (in 1535) of £22. In spite of this it maintained the discipline of the order to a high standard and was called by Dafydd ap Gwilym 'Lan falch llugan' - proud Llanllugan. As late as 1530 a nun from the Augustinian house of Limebrook in the Welsh borders had heard that a stricter and more spiritually fulfilling rule was maintained at Llanllugan. So great was its superiority over that to which she was accustomed that she wished to transfer to the latter. When the house was suppresed in 1536 there were three nuns in the convent.

The buildings

There are no remains of the actual house at Llanllugan but the church used by the nuns survives a little to the north of, and above, the presumed site of the conventual buildings. The church comprised a simple rectangular building 19 m long and 8 m wide and survives, as such, to this day. Hasland (*Buildings of Wales*, Penguin Series) thinks it possible that the church may once have been longer. Apart from the main doorway to the nave there are blocked doorways on both the north and south side of the church nearer the east end. Either of these could have been connected with the nuns' use of the building and their access from the conventual buildings. The present building preserves several features dating from the 15th century and a font which may be of the 13th century.

Further reading

M.C. Jones, Some Account of Llanllugan Nunnery. *Monmouthshire Antiquary* Vol 2 1969.

Llanllyr
Cistercian house of nuns

Llanllyr was the second foundation in Wales of a house for nuns following the Cistercian order. It followed shortly after the collapse of the house at Llansantfraed in Elfael (*q.v.*) and it is possible that some nuns from the earlier foundation removed there. Llanllyr was founded by the Lord Rhys about 1180 in the Aeron valley between Lampeter and Aberaeron. It was a daughter house of Strata Florida which latter house appears to have regarded the nunnery as little more than a cell or grange of its abbey. Gerald of Wales noted (late 12th century) that the house was 'small and poor' but by repute the 16 nuns who made up the convent were of high rank. In the 13th century Llanllyr suffered at the hands of both friends and enemies. On the death of the Lord Rhys, Strata Florida took to itself some of the nunnery's lands. Although Llanllyr had 1200 acres under the plough that land was desperately poor. The house was assessed in 1291 at a paltry £7.

The convent had suffered from damage during the later Welsh wars but Strata Florida had collected the money owed as compensation on behalf of its little daughter house and little of the £25 owing may have reached Llanllyr. At the suppression in 1536 Llanllyr's income was valued at £57, not rich but sufficient to maintain a convent of nuns which, it is thought, was somewhat diminished in number from earlier days.

There are no remains of the nunnery at Llanllyr but antiquarians of the last century noted that a white cottage that still stood in the vicinity belonged to it. This cottage would have been in present-day Ystrad Aeron.

Llansantffraed in Elfael
Cistercian house of nuns

Llansantffraed was the first house for nuns of the Cistercian order to be founded in Wales and had a short, disastrous career. Elfael was a small province of mid Wales over which Powys, from time to time, claimed overlordship. The great abbey of Powys was Strata Marcella which was founded in 1170. Llansantffraed nunnery was established in Elfael as a daughter house of Strata Marcella but Gerald of Wales recorded an unsavoury relationship between the two houses. It seems that Enoch, the first abbot of Strata Marcella, eloped with one of the nuns shortly after the convent had been established. Seeing the error of his ways, however, he returned to his abbey a much chastened man. There he received the 'discipline of incontinence' from three priests. Llansantffraed, having got off to such a bad start, does not appear to have carried on and subseqeuntly disappeared from the records. Its entire history, therefore, is contained in the short period between about 1172 and 1190.

Llantarnam Abbey
Cistercian abbey

History
Llantarnam Abbey was a daughter house of Strata Florida and was alone, therefore, in the south-east corner of Wales, as a truly Welsh monastery. The founder, about 1179, was a local Welsh ruler, Hywel ap Iorwerth of Caerleon. The abbey was formerly known as Caerleon Abbey and quite probably the site of the original foundation was nearer that town. D. H. Williams (*Monmouthshire Antiquary* Vol 2) proposes that a transfer may have taken place about 1272 and notes the use of the phrase 'old abbey' thereafter in some documents pertaining to Llantarnam.

The abbey was endowed with extensive mountain pastures stretching away westwards towards the Rhondda. In its early days the convent was some 60 strong (probably including lay brethren) and from the outset was notably Welsh in character. It was never wealthy and was valued in 1291 at only £19. By that date it had already been in dispute with Margam and Tintern Abbeys and also, more notably, with Gilbert de Clare who was Earl of Gloucester. Goldcliff Priory, just a few miles away, also suffered through its dealings with de Clare. About 1272 Llantarnam found itself in dire straits because the earl had apparently relieved the abbey of that little burden of worldy wealth which it had already acquired. By the early 14th century the convent appears to have been at a third of its former strength but further vicissitudes were in store. At the end of that century an accidental fire extensively damaged the buildings and their contents and for many years the monks were engaged in raising funds to make good their losses. Worse was to come in the Glyndwr rebellion. At that time the convent, and particularly the abbot, appears to have been fiercely in favour of the independent Welsh cause. The abbot, John ap Hywel, was involved in an attack on Usk and during that engagement was killed by the English.

In the last century of its existence Llantarnam was much engaged in maintaining its traditional position and manorial rights. It may be as a result of its involvement with Glyndwr that these rights were threatened. As the Dissolution approached the abbey's lands were extensively commuted by leasing. The Dissolution took place in 1536 when just six monks were left and the abbey was valued at £81.

The buildings
Since there are no remains of the abbey we have no idea as to what buildings existed. D. H. Williams (*op. cit.*) points out that manuscripts give evidence of a Lady Chapel, bell tower, cemetery and cloister. Therefore, we have reason to believe that a substantial monastic establishment existed and not one seriously curtailed by political and financial constraints as at Cymer and Cwmhir further north. Although there are early connections with Caerleon the later abbey was definitely on the site of the modern 'Llantarnam Abbey'. The present building is a creation of the early Victorian period but incorporates a little masonry which may date from the monastic period.

Further reading
D.H. Williams, Llantarnam Abbey. *Monmouthshire Antiquary* Vol 2.

Llanthony

Augustinian priory of St John the Baptist

History

Thrusting through the undergrowth, deep in a valley of the Black Mountains, William de Lacy came upon the ruined chapel of St David, a symbol of the old Celtic past. Although a retainer and relation to the Lord of Ewyas, he resolved to spend the rest of his life as a hermit in this peaceful spot. A few years later, in 1103, when this act of devotion was more widely known, he was joined by Ernisius, a priest with the highest secular connections. Together they established a small community and built a church dedicated in 1108. About 10 years later the community regularised its existence by adopting the new, reforming Augustinian Order. Canons from the existing houses of the order also came to join the convent. The priory was now patronised by the mightiest in the land, namely King Henry I and Queen Matilda.

The accession of Stephen to the throne heralded a period of civil disorder in England and a chance for South Wales to re-assert its independence. Within a year the priory's position had become untenable and the canons withdrew to Gloucester in 1136 where their former prior was now bishop. This led to the setting up of a new priory at Gloucester from which the original Llanthony in the Black Mountains became a place of pilgrimage. The monastery in the mountains was deteriorating into an empty shell but by 1175 it was found possible to bring new life to Llanthony. The priory had been enriched with endowments in Ireland and the community rapidly recovered its original strength and vitality. Within 50 years a magnificent new church had been erected of which there are substantial remains today. Gerald of Wales, who visited the priory in the late twelfth century, found the place idyllic but noted with some distaste the material comforts available to the canons.

The life of the community apparently ran smoothly through the vicissitudes of the final

LLANTHONY PRIORY

1. *West range survives more substantially than shown but remains are absorbed in the hotel*
2. *Frater, remains of basement can be seen on left as the site is entered*
3. *Further buildings of the east range, some remains showing but not investigated as yet*
4. *Chapter house*

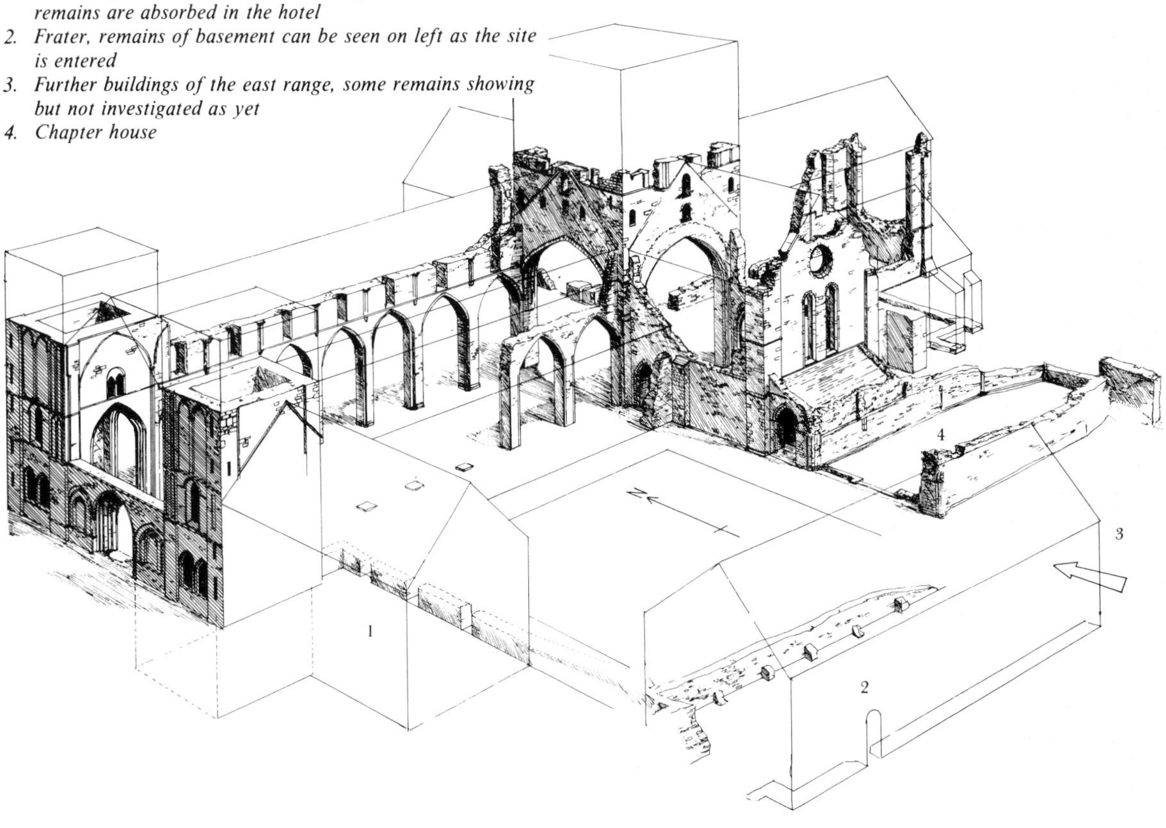

Llanthony Priory in an early 19th century print.

Welsh wars until about 1270 when it was caught up in the final upheaval. Some canons were killed, others ran off and possessions were taken. There is some evidence that the buildings themselves were in poor condition but in spite of this the priory was valued at £233 in the assessment of 1291.

Throughout the following century the canons maintained their house and their rights, sometimes with considerable forcefulness. But it was a difficult time for all Welsh monasteries. The Glyndwr rebellion caused special difficulties for houses in south-east Wales and Llanthony, being very much of English 'pedigree', suffered considerable ruination. From 1400 onwards the priory's fortunes suffered as a result and by 1481 it had become a cell of the alternative Llanthony at Gloucester. At the Dissolution the priory's annual income was assessed at just £112 with a prior and three canons in residence. It was dissolved in 1538.

The buildings

Llanthony's position is one of outstanding beauty, even by Welsh standards. Set deep in the Black Mountains, 10 miles north of Abergavenny, it was ideal for the contemplative life. Llanthony was the largest Augustinian house in Wales and was built on conventional lines. The church was of cruciform shape with aisles north and south of the nave. A chapel led off each transept. At the west end of the nave the aisles terminated in towers - a feature unique in Welsh monastic buildings - but then, as has been seen, this was more of an English colony in Wales. The conventual buildings followed the normal pattern with the frater running along the length of the south range. In the east range a fine chapter house, stone vaulted and with a narrowing east end, was the principal building. Notable, between chapter house and transept, was the vaulted slype. Around this area is

Chepstow Church.

An important early 19th century print of Pill Priory by Gastineau. Something of the full height of the original tower is shown together with indications of the presbytery roof. The cottages to the left, on the site of the conventional buildings, appear to preserve some details of medieval age and cannot be entirely discounted as representing remains of the east range.

Neath Abbey. The base of the night stairs in the south transept. The stone handrail is inserted into a west wall of the transept.

Monkton Priory (Pembroke). The restored east end of the church. The conventional buildings were to the right.

evidence of reconstruction of the south transept.

Today, Llanthony presents some of the most picturesque ruins in Wales and is now in the hands of Cadw. The principal interest is the church with substantial remains of the crossing tower, nave and the splendid west front. The towers here are missing their top storey. The conventual buildings of the west range are in use as a hotel, ironically appropriate. The original height of the range can be seen by the sill marks high up on the south-west tower of the church. The east range is largely ruined south of the slype and needs further investigation. The chapter house, however, has some worthwhile remains. The cellar of the frater is discernible from the indications of vaulting in the wall as one enters the abbey precinct.

Further reading

O.E. Craster, *Llanthony Priory*. HMSO 1963.

Margam
Cistercian

History

Margam became the richest house of Cistercian monks in Wales and its buildings clearly reflected that wealth in their considerable magnificence. In 1147 Robert FitzRoy, Earl of Gloucester and the eldest of Henry I's natural sons, gave a parcel of land to Bernard of Clairvaux to establish a monastery of Cistercian monks. It is possible that the first foundation was at Pendar, hidden deeper in the highlands to the north but the site at Margam was ideal for the economic future of the abbey. It was adjacent to the extensive sheepwalks, rich lowlands, the sea and coal seams. In its life it acquired enormous estates, nearly 7000 acres by 1291 when it was valued at £181, somewhat less than neighbouring Neath Abbey. By that time the church had already been rebuilt to something of the appearance that we discern today.

MARGAM ABBEY

1. *Nave, now incorporated into modern parish church*
2. *Monks' entrance to church from cloister*
3. *Vestibule to chapter house*
4. *Chapter house*
5. *Possible reredorter*
6. *Orangery now on site of south range*

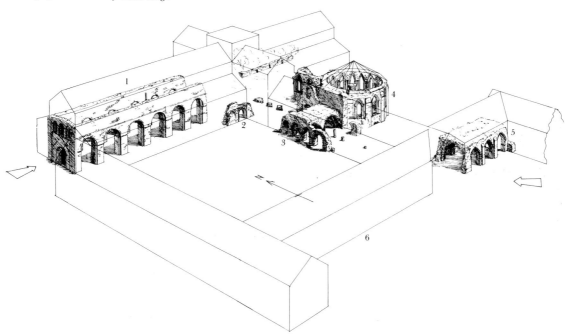

Margam Abbey — the doorway in the south-east corner of the presbytery.

Gerald of Wales had noted the 'charitable deeds' of the convent for which it gained fame but it was essentially an English house of monks and not favoured by the Welsh. Two kings, Henry I and John, stayed at Margam with satisfaction, a fact that did not ingratiate the convent into the political sympathies of local militant leaders, particularly Morgan Gam, who repeatedly ravaged the abbey's possessions. In 1223 and 1224 over 1000 sheep were slaughtered and two granges destroyed. Such devastations continued nearly up to the death of Morgan Gam in 1240. Ironically, he was buried in the abbey precinct. Other hardships came from the Cistercians themselves when there were differences with both Neath and Llantarnam about the extent of respective sheep walks.

After the Welsh wars difficulties were not eased. Gilbert de Clare seized lands belonging to the abbey and by 1366 it could barely support the 38 monks in the convent. Margam was severely hit by the Black Death after which there was an increased tendency to farm the estates. Although the abbey became increasingly impoverished its value of £266 in 1383 would have been the envy of other Welsh houses. It did not, therefore, escape the ravages of the Glyndwr rebellion after which it was found to be utterly destroyed with the abbot and his monks wandering like vagabonds . This was the nadir of the abbey's fortunes and, though it never really recovered, there was some restoration work in the middle of the fifteenth century. In the sixteenth century the abbey seems to have become more Welsh in character but, unfortunately, rather more decadent as well. Although valued at the Dissolution at £181 there were just eight monks in the convent. The house was suppressed in 1536.

The buildings

Margam Abbey was built at the very edge of the Welsh uplands where they pile up against the Bristol Channel east of present-day Port Talbot. Famed of its wealth, it was among the largest abbeys in Wales, comparable with Neath and Tintern. The layout of the buildings was perfectly normal, a large church with cloisters and conventual buildings to the south. The church was cruciform in shape with aisles either side of the nave and presbytery. The east end of the church was rebuilt in the twelfth century in the Early English style. In each of the short transepts there was space for two chapels. In plan the church at Margam was strikingly similar to that at Neath. In respect of the extant buildings, however, Margam predates Neath which was substantially rebuilt in the thirteenth century. From that periods dates the 12-sided chapter house at Margam which replaced an earlier vaulted structure contained within the east range. The room for the sacristy, as at Neath, was divided so that the western half could be used as a book store. The south range of the conventual building is only slightly known from limited excavations but it appears that the frater was on an east-west axis occupying the greater part of the length of the range.

It is most unusual for a Cistercian church to remain in use but at Margam six bays of the original nave have been incorporated into what looks, from the outside, a far from contemporaneous building. The massive arcade, on rectangular piers, is somewhat reminiscent of the Benedictine priory church at Chepstow. The west front of the church preserves the late Norman windows and doorway but is otherwise very much restored. Other remains are visible but not at present accessible to the public. They consist of portions of walling of the east end of the church (some interesting details and doorways), part of the south transept and remains of the east range. Outstanding in the last is the quite beautiful chapter house which, although unroofed, retains excellent masonry and is a most pleasing structure. There are attractive details also in the doorway leading from the cloister to the monks' choir. The vaulted structure south of the chapter house has been interpreted as leading to the infirmary but may well have been associated with the reredorter arrangements. The south range occupied the site now occupied by the famous orangery.

Further reading

A. Leslie Evans, *Margam Abbey*, Port Talbot 1958.

Monmouth

Benedictine priory

History

About 1070 William FitzOsbern built a castle in the Welsh settlement of Monmouth. Later the Breton, Guihenoc of Monmouth, endowed the abbey of St Florent, near Saumur in his native France, with the church of St Mary at Monmouth together with sufficient lands and rights to make it possible to maintain a full convent of monks. The endowment was confirmed in 1086 and within 20 years a priory had been established. The priory church was built onto the parish church and dedicated in 1101 or 1102. At first there were seven monks and a prior in the convent. Very little is known of its early days but between 1263 and 1268 it appears to have been in some financial difficulties and a great deal of its extensive properties were sold or mortgaged. In 1291 it was valued at nearly £86 and owned 480 acres of estates. The town of Monmouth was growing steadily and the priory also possessed burgesses within the walls. It was also responsible for two hospitals in the town. The annual payment to the mother house of £6 13s 4d was the highest such payment made by the numerous alien priories of south east Wales.

In 1309 both the monks and parishioners were outraged when a band of Welshmen under Griffith Goht murdered a man who had escaped from the castle prison and taken refuge in the church. A similar assault took place in 1318 on the vicar and clerk of the church but not, this time, with fatal results.

Being an alien priory, Monmouth had a difficult history during the 14th century but when the seizure of alien priories took place in 1414 matters actually improved. Like other such priories in Gwent (Chepstow, Abergavenny and Goldcliff) it became a denizen (native) priory with an independent English convent technically subject to God's House College, Cambridge. It had also suffered indirectly as a result of the Glyndwr rebellion because of the devastation to the tithe properties it held in Herefordshire.

1. *Spire, a rebuilding of the mid 18th century*
2. *Tower with 12th century respond of arch on south east corner*
3. *Speculative reconstruction of monastic portion of church inferred from prints and position of conventional buildings*
4. *Geoffrey's Window*
5. *North range as suggested by early prints*

At the Dissolution the priory's income was assessed at just £56 and the church was almost falling down, so poor was its condition. The convent comprised just two monks, one boarding in the town and the prior living out of the town. The priory was dissolved in 1540, the priory church was then stripped of its lead and left to ruin.

The buildings

Although St Mary's Church stands today, nothing remains of the priory church except the tower and spire at the west end of the nave which date from the monastic period. The spire was rebuilt in about 1750. Inside the church the respond of an arch that constituted the first bay of the nave shows that the arcade was in the Norman (Romanesque) style of massive round piers and arches. These few remains, together with clues from surrounding buildings and one or two old prints, do give us some idea of the appearance of the priory church.

The church, shortly after the suppression, was described as beautiful and of three aisles with a ruined priory section adjoining the east end. The drawing by Dinely for the *Duke of Beaufort's Progress through Wales*

Geoffrey's window, Monmouth. Early 19th century.

(1684) reflects this description and shows the priory church ruins with what appear to be Romanesque spires and arches. A large arch immediately adjacent to the parish nave suggests a crossing with two transepts supporting a tower. Two smaller arches to the east suggest the presbytery with side chapels or aisles, rather reminiscent of nearby Abergavenny Priory. The conventual buildings were to the north of the church and a particularly fine oriel window survives from these. A little of the layout can be inferred from this portion which clearly looked out from the north range. An illustration in Cox's *Tour of Monmouthshire* suggests that more of the conventual buildings existed then. An inventory made at the time of the Dissolution indicates that these could have been a frater, buttery, kitchen, bishop's chamber and auditor's chamber.

The principal survival from the priory, therefore, is now the oriel window known as 'Geoffrey's Window' which was part of the north range of the conventual buildings. Early prints reveal that this window was on the gable end of a building projecting northwards from that range.

Further reading

W. Bagnal-Oakely, Monmouth, *Arch. Camb* 1896.

Neath
Cistercian abbey

History

Neath deserves particular attention because there is some evidence that it was the most noteworthy ecclesiastical building in Wales in terms of architecture. Its origins date from the first Norman invasion of South Wales and in the eyes of the Welsh the foundation was another facet of that invasion. It was founded in 1129 when Richard de Granville granted an enormous tract of land between the River Neath and the western boundary of the old princedom of Morgannwg (between the Neath and Tawe Rivers) to the abbey of Savigny in Normandy. The following year the monks of that house established an abbey very close to the Norman castle which predated the nearby castle of Neath town. At this stage Neath

was not Cisterican but so similar was the order of the houses of Savigny (Basingwerk was the other Welsh house of that Order) to that of the Cistercian houses that in 1147 the two orders merged.

Also in 1147, Margam Abbey was established a few miles to the west. Margam was able to secure extensive rights of pasturage which neighboured those of Neath and this led to friction between the two houses. So severe was this during the twelfth and thirteenth centuries that at one stage Neath Abbey considered transferring to Somerset. The proposed site, already owned by Neath Abbey, was too close to Cleeve Abbey (also Cistercian) to make the prospects of peace and success any better there. In any case, Neath's sheep pastures were more than adequate to its needs and there was additional income to be had, particularly in later years, from coal and iron ore. The abbey also traded around the Bristol Channel using its own vessels. So the Somerset property was sold and new lands acquired in Gower in its place.

Another reason for the monks of Neath to be less than enthusiastic about their Welsh home was the hostility of the native population. During the Welsh wars the abbey was attacked, servants were killed and livestock destroyed. In spite of these difficulties Neath was valued, in 1291, at £236 making it the wealthiest Cistercian house in Wales. There were nearly 5000 sheep on the pastures and over 200 head of cattle. It was at this time that the abbey was rebuilt and the new church appeared which was later to be described by Leland as the fairest in Wales. The new buildings were almost immediately plundered and severely damaged in one of the flare-ups of Welsh resistance in the early 14th century. In 1326 the abbey was one of the last places Edward II stayed in before his unfortunate demise. The rest of the 14th and 15th centuries saw a slow decline in Neath's fortunes. It suffered from floods, high tides and, finally, the aftermath of the Glyndwr rebellion.

In the last 50 years of its life the abbey underwent a partial renaissance. Essential repairs were carried out and fine new apartments were built for the abbot. In the last years before the Dissolution this was the renowned figure of Leyshon Thomas. The final dissolution of Neath Abbey took place in 1539. At that time there were seven monks

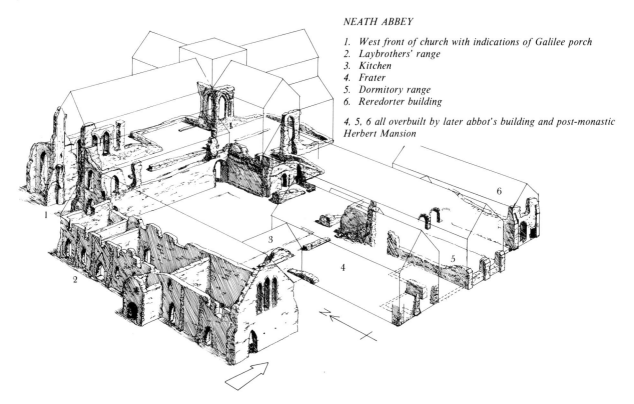

apart from Leyshon Thomas. The annual income had previously been assessed at just £132, a reflection of the vicissitudes of its latter years.

The buildings

The abbey was established close by the tidal reaches of the Afon Nedd (Neath River) winding sinuously across the wide level floor of the valley. Immediately above the abbey precincts rise the gentle foothills of the Fforest Fawr and the Black Mountain. Set amidst the commercial and industrial developments of today a special effort of the imagination is required to picture the simplicity of its site 700 years ago. It was not as secluded, however, as its Cistercian counterparts. Close by was the motte of the first Neath Castle together with the seeds of the first town of Neath. Within a hundred years, however, town and castle were developing further upstream on the opposite (left) bank of the river.

It seems probable that the first church was erected slightly south of the later church roughly along the line of the north cloister walk. Although much smaller than the thirteenth-century church it was comparable in size to the first church at Tintern and other contemporaneous Cistercian abbeys. The conventual buildings followed the normal plan but the early arrangement of the south range is not known to us, the present remains of the frater show it following the later style with its length at right angles to the line of the south cloister walk. The frater, the monks' lodgings, the chapter house and parlour were all complete by the end of the 13th century at which time the new church was being erected. This was the building that so impressed Leland more than any other of its type in Wales more than 300 years later. The new cruciform church had north and south aisles, an ambulatory around the presbytery and two chapels in each transept. The west end of the nave had a Galilee porch added. In the later years of the abbey the abbot took over a significant portion of the monks' lodging rooms. When the abbey was taken over by Sir John Herbert after the Dissolution he developed the abbot's rooms and extended his own mansion over the south east corner of the conventual buildings. In more recent years, before the ruins were taken into the care of the Ministry of Works (subsequently Cadw) they were much blighted by industrial activity.

Today the ruins present some of the most complete remains of a Cistercian abbey to be found in Wales. Much, however, is badly ruined. The height of the church may be roughly guessed from the ruined corners of the west front but little else remains of its glory. In the south transept the night stairs to the monks' dormitory remain partially intact with the stone handrail set in the wall, a rare survival. The east range is utterly ruined except in the southern part where the vaulted undercroft of the dormitory survives. The base of the day stairs from the dormitory may also be seen. The reredorter and drainage arrangements reveal interesting details. The western range, the oldest surviving part of the abbey, is substantially intact with a fourteenth-century gateway leading through the range into the lane abutting the cloister. The doorway from the cloister into the church has beautiful moulding, an indication of what treasures have been lost.

A short distance from the ruins, the abbey gatehouse survives, in part, by the main road leading into Skewen.

Further reading

W. de G. Birch, *Neath Abbey*, 1902. The definitive work on the history of Neath Abbey. L.A.S. Butler, *Neath Abbey*, 1976. The HMSO Guide.

Pembroke (Monkton)

Benedictine priory
Church of St Nicholas

History

Pembroke Priory was placed, like Kidwelly, a discreet distance from the great castle of its patron across a narrow stretch of water. It was founded by Arnulph de Montgomery, brother of the enormously powerful Earl of Shrewsbury, in 1098. The site may have been that of a previous Celtic church. Arnulph made a grant to the abbey of St Martin of Seez and the priory was founded only a year after the castle at Pembroke had been started. Because of the French connection the priory was designated as 'alien' once the conflict with France began in the 14th century.

The little that is known of the history of Pembroke Priory reflects the troubled times of which it was part. When Gerald of Wales visited the priory in 1171 the Sheriff of Pembroke was determined to show contempt for the Welsh cleric and promptly removed eight yoke of oxen from the priory's land. A century later, when Archbishop Pecham was surveying the conditions in Welsh monasteries, the prior was found sorely wanting. His unharnessed sexual appetite and other 'enormous and incredible offences' had ruined the reputation of the priory and scandalised the neighbourhood. Pecham had no option but to depose the wayward prior.

For all its powerful patronage Pembroke was only valued at £19 in 1291. As an alien priory it was bound to suffer various forfeitures in the course of the following century but survived dissolution with other such houses to become the property of St Alban's Abbey in 1443. At the time there were probably no more than four monks and a prior at Pembroke. Before the final Dissolution in 1539 it was valued at just £57.

The buildings

The priory occupied a little promontory of level land overlooking the waterway between itself and the castle. The plan of the conventual buildings is not known but faint remains have indicated that they were built north of the church. The church itself was exceptionally long (53 m) compared with its width (9 m), consisting of an aisleless nave for parish use with the monks' church occupying what is now the chancel. Between the two churches a stone screen would have separated conventual from secular activities. On the south side of the nave, occupying a 'transeptal' position, stands a tall tower of Tudor date and Pembrokeshire style. Opposite this 'transept' is a pointed arch matching that giving access to the space under the tower. Next to the space where one would have expected this north transept, and east of it, the vestry has traces of a vaulted undercroft and a stairway leading above. East of this is the 'Prior's Chapel', an unusual feature suggesting unexpected complexity in the conventual arrangements attaching to the church.

The exterior of the north side of the nave, now heavily buttressed, reveals two windows of twelfth-century date, the later church seems

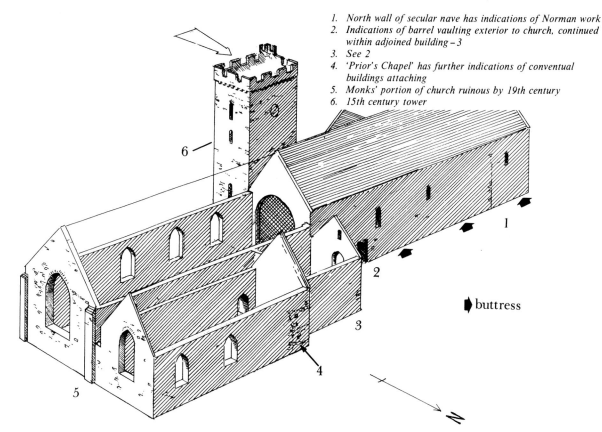

1. *North wall of secular nave has indications of Norman work*
2. *Indications of barrel vaulting exterior to church, continued within adjoined building – 3*
3. *See 2*
4. *'Prior's Chapel' has further indications of conventual buildings attaching*
5. *Monks' portion of church ruinous by 19th century*
6. *15th century tower*

buttress

to have been built within the line of the original wall. At the east end of this length of walling are further traces of the connection with the conventual buildings.

Early depictions of the priory might be expected to cast some light on the arrangements of the conventual buildings but the depiction of these in the Speed map is particularly unhelpful and misleading. Since his drawing of the church bears no resemblance to our knowledge of its appearance at any stage of its history we must ignore his depiction of other parts of the priory. The drawing by Buck from the following (18th) century is rather more helpful and indicates an interesting tower-like structure at the junction of the monastic buildings with the church. This may possibly be a leftover from an earlier period or could have contained a stairway leading to an upper floor.

In the 19th century the monastic remains at Monkton church were in ruins and declining rapidly. It is tempting to think that the restoration was heavy handed but the alternative at the time was probably demolition and we must, therefore, regard ourselves as fortunate with what we have. Indeed, with a church of such narrowness and length the restoration, completed in 1910, had difficult aesthetic problems and managed to produce a dignified and convincing structure from the ruins. Photographs of the original structure are displayed on the walls of the church. The restored sedilia and three tombs within the 'chancel' are particularly worthy of note.

Further reading

E. Laws. Notes on the alien Benedictine Priory of St Nicholas and St John the Evangelist in Monkton, Pembroke. *Arch. Camb.* 1909.

Penmon and Puffin Island

Augustinian priory from a Celtic monastery

History

In the traditions of Welsh monasticism it was not unusual to have twin settlements such as at Penmon and Priestholm (now Puffin Island). Because the latter, as an offshore island, was so suitable for the eremitic way of life we may suppose that it was the original focus of the monastery that was established, traditionally, by Cynlas in the 6th century. It may be that the island was a place of withdrawal, however, from the less austere life of the mainland settlement at Penmon. This was reputedly founded by the old 'British' King Maelgwn. Little is known of the history of the Celtic community but it certainly developed as a clas and the several

cells on the island bear witness to that period. The mainland church was named after Seiriol, brother of Cynlas and the first 'prior' of the house. Ynys Seiriol (Seiriol's Island) is the Welsh name for Puffin Island.

The Celtic community survived the ravages of the Vikings in the 10th century and was still active when the Normans were making inroads into Wales. The church at Penmon, although of Norman age and character, is thus of exceptional interest because it was built for a monastery that was purely Welsh. Evidence suggests that it was not until the early 13th century that the community adopted the official Augustinian Order, a change that did not greatly alter the way of life of the monastery. At this time Penmon was granted to the priory of Priestholm which effectively led to Penmon becoming the active centre of the community. With the adoption of the Augus-

PENMON PRIORY

1. *The canons' portion of the church now rebuilt on original foundations*
2. *Transepts were substantially rebuilt in the 19th century*
3. *Frater and dormitory*
4. *Warming house and kitchen added shortly before the priory was suppressed*

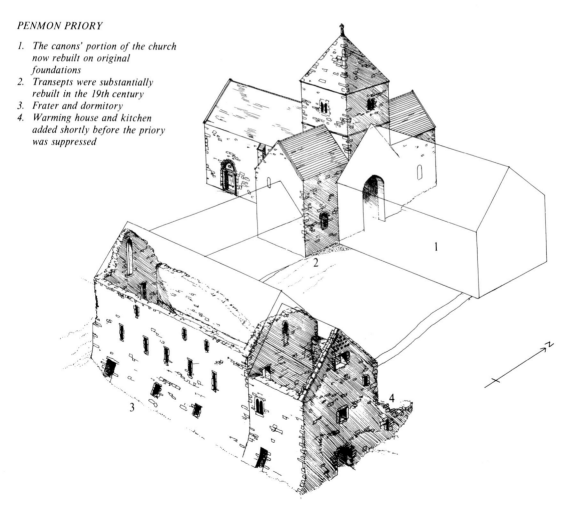

tinian Order it appears that more typically Norman buildings were erected to accommodate the convent.

The priory was never prosperous or large and suffered a number of setbacks after the loss of Welsh independence before which it had been favoured by the Welsh royal family. It was burnt in the conflict of 1282 and received £46 compensation. Shortly after we find the convent suffering under a wayward and lustful prior. Penmon was placed too near the burgeoning Edwardian settlement and castle of Beaumaris to avoid its influence. The priory came to be used as a staging post for political emissaries travelling to and from Ireland, this was a substantial burden for a small house to bear. By the beginning of the 15th century the priory was governed by English priors who owned burgages in Beaumaris town. These priors were increasingly secular in their interests and probably resided in the town for at least some of the time. It is likely, also, that by the 16th century members of the convent had broken the rule of celibacy.

The priory was dissolved in 1536 with two canons in residence. Its assessed income of £40 made it just about the poorest house of Augustinians in Wales, a sad end to one of the longest lived monasteries in the Principality.

The buildings

Penmon Priory rests in a shallow valley close to the extreme eastern corner of Anglesey. It is a fairly confined spot and the conventual buildings formed a compact group. The plan of the original church is not known, that structure having been sacked and burned by the Danes and replaced by the Welsh. The present nave, 12 m long, dates from about 1140 and displays many features from the Welsh (pre-Norman) period. The church was cruciform with the canons' section occupying the eastern half. This portion of the church was, apparently, rebuilt and a range of conventual buildings added at the time of the adoption of the Augustinian order. The conventual buildings were attached to the south transept, the 'Prior's house' in the west range, the frater and dormitory comprising the south range with a warming house and kitchen added in the 16th century. Internal details in the south transept point to the west range consisting of a small building with no direct access to the church.

The monastic settlement on Puffin Island stood within an earlier Celtic 'cashel', in this case an oval enclosure some 100 m across. The tiny church would not have exceeded 17 m in length. It comprised a short nave to which was added a little tower 8 m high, which has been dated as 12th century. There are indications of a chancel and also of a building extending south from the tower. North west of the church earlier cells were built both within and without the cashel, adjoining the boundary wall. They were mostly rectangular and of varying sizes.

Today, Penmon church presents a valuable survival from the Celtic age. From that period the nave and transepts survive with splendid details in the tower arch and in the carved tympanum over the nave doorway. Within the

PENMON PRIORY
The doorway to the nave belonging to the pre-conquest period (c. 1150) with a dragon motif on the tympanum.

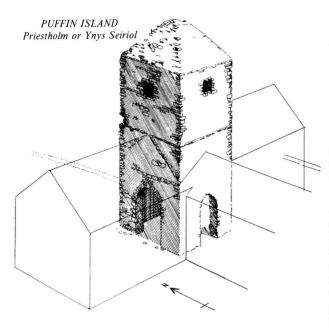

PUFFIN ISLAND
Priestholm or Ynys Seiriol

nave stands a fine Celtic cross. The arcades in the wall of the south transept are of particular note. The chancel is a thorough rebuilding of the original monastic end of the church, completed in 1885. The west range seen today is not the monastic building but the south range survives reasonably intact.

Further reading

A.D. Carr, The Priory of Penmon, *Journal of Ecclesiastical History*, 1986. A definitive history of the house.
RACHM Anglesey. *Penmon and Puffin Island.* A complete description of the buildings.

Pill

Church of St Budoc and the Blessed Virgin

History

Like the cathedral at St Davids, though on a far smaller scale, the priory at Pill nestles deep in a valley hidden from the eyes of sea-farers in nearby Milford Haven. It belonged to the trio of Pembrokeshire houses that followed the Order of Tiron, the other two being St Dogmaels (the mother house) and Caldey. The date of its foundation is far from clear, surely before 1200 but some time after Caldey (1117). The foundation is attributed to Adam de la Roche who gave the priory sufficient endowments to support a proper convent of monks. In time the house acquired over 1300 acres of land but remained very small and relatively poor. In 1291 it was valued at just £21.

PILL PRIORY

1. Speculative reconstruction of nave
2. South wall of south transept connecting with conventual buildings
3. Tentative reconstruction of east range

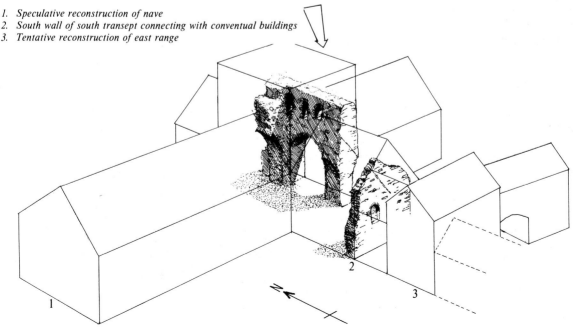

In the mid 14th century the prior complained that a descendant of Adam de la Roche had done great damage to both the priory and its convent. This was an ironic blow since the Flemish de la Roches, recognised as founders, were generally buried at Pill.

The priory apparently led a quiet life and, at a visitation in 1504, was found to be in good order with the church recently repaired by the prior. At that time there were five monks besides the prior, a small but well disciplined convent. It was dissolved in 1536 having its income valued at £52 and with three monks in residence.

The buildings

The priory was built on level land on a site restricted by the Hubberton Pill and the steep sides of the valley. Many authorities state that Pill Priory was diminutive in size but, although certainly not large, the extant remains suggest that the church was not insubstantial. The width of the nave was probably about 11 m, of the same order of size as the mother church at St Dogmael's. There are indications of transepts to north and south and neighbouring buildings, including the nearby inn, are ranged in roughly the pattern that might be expected of the conventual buildings. We can only infer from this that the conventual ranges were to the south of the church and that the existing buildings may be on their foundations.

All that remains today is the crumbling chancel arch with a wall of the crossing tower above, pierced by three simple lights. The south transept can be traced and appears to be partially incorporated into an adjacent building. What may possibly have been a doorway to the night stairs from the dormitory is visible.

St Dogmael's
Abbey of the Order of Tiron
Dedicated to the Blessed Virgin Mary

History

The Order of Tiron was a reforming Benedictine order, similar to those of Cîteaux (Cistercian) and Savigny, that flourished in the early 13th century. In fact, the Order of Tiron originated close to the abbey of Savigny from which the abbeys of Neath and Basingwerk were established. In England and Wales the monks of Tiron were not notably successful. Of the seven houses established, three were in or close to Hampshire and three were in Pembrokeshire. The latter were the most successful, doubtless because the main house at St Dogmael's acquired the status of an abbey at an early date thus giving a non alien character to the Pembrokeshire houses.

Martin of Tiron, who died before 1086, may have wished to establish a monastery in Cemais, a large district of west Wales of which he and his son Robert were conquerors. Martin's widow, Geva, and Robert seem to have treasured his wishes and founded the priory at St Dogmael's in 1113 or shortly thereafter, close to the site of an old Celtic monastery. Within the choir of the new church they buried Martin.

In 1120 the abbot of Tiron agreed to St Dogmael's becoming an abbey but the house was still closely tied to Tiron which retained the important right to elect the abbot of St Dogmael's. The abbey was endowed with Caldey Island, a gift from Geva, where a dependent priory was shortly established. Two more dependent priories were established at Pill, near Milford Haven and at Glascerry in southern Ireland.

The evidence of the building remains suggests that the abbey may have suffered some destruction at the end of the 12th century when the Lord Rhys asserted his control over the Norman holdings of much of south-west Wales. There followed, however, a period of relative calm for St Dogmael's and to this period may be attributed the principal extant remains of the church which was, presumably, rebuilt at that time. In the Taxation of 1291, St Dogmael's was assessed at £58 and held 720 acres of land. The low value placed on the house together with substantial rebuilding that took place in the early 14th century

ST DOGMAEL'S

1. Nave of Church
2. Crossing, separated from nave by stone screen and pulpitum
3. Presbytery
4. Crypt
5. Apsidal Chapel, blocked
6. Chapter House
7. Infirmary
8. Passage through east range
9. Frater
10. West range
11. Probable site of guest house
A. Area greatly confused by post-monastic buildings

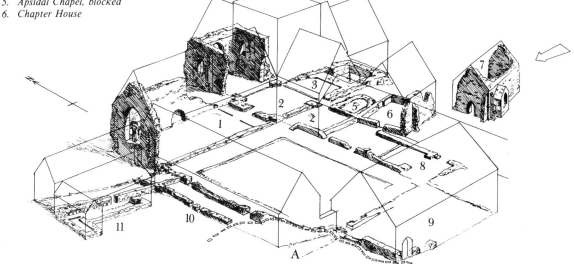

The infirmary of the Abbey of St Dogmael's.

may be the result of a further destruction of the abbey that had taken place at the end of the Welsh wars. Little more is known of the history of the abbey and at the suppression in 1536 it was valued at £87 with eight monks apart from the abbot.

The buildings

St Dogmael's stands on a sloping site overlooking the Teifi estuary from the south side. The plan of the abbey was straightforward, a cruciform church with the conventual buildings ranged to the south in the normal pattern. The nave was originally conceived with two aisles but only the south aisle was completed. Eventually the south aisle was dismantled and the north cloister walk occupied from space made available. The nave was separated from the presbytery by a pulpitum with a central doorway and in front of this was a stone rood screen. An apsed chapel extended from the south transept whilst the north transept is a rebuilding of the early 16th century. From early in its history the abbey had an infirm-, ary (13th century) but this was placed so that when a new chapter house was built extending from the east range it had to be skewed to the north. The fourteenth-century frater extended along the length of the south range. Beyond the west range and the west front of the church was placed the guest house.

The site is now in the care of Cadw and is approached, picturesquely, through the village. Passing through the entrance gate the east range is arrived at by passing the infirmary building. At the east end of the church a small thirteenth-century crypt can be seen, an unusual feature in Welsh monastic churches. The principal remains of the church are of the north transept and the north and west walls of the nave. In the north transept can be seen remnants of the vaulted ceiling with the corbels from which the vaulting sprang. In an adjacent base of a crossing pier can be seen the bottom of the stair leading onto the pulpitum. The most complete of the remaining buildings is the infirmary, a survival unique in Welsh abbeys. It is a simple, rectangular building of the late 13th century with a small vaulted extension to the south. Much of the conventual buildings can be discerned from the foundations remaining, which are extensive.

Further reading
C.A. Ralegh Radford, *St Dogmael's Abbey* HMSO. As always, concise and authoritative.
E.M. Pritchard, *History of St Dogmael's Abbey*. The definitive history.

Strata Florida
Cistercian abbey

History

Compared with Cistercian houses in England, Strata Florida was insignificant if judged by its wealth. Within Wales, however, few religious houses were of comparable significance. Strata Florida, although not rich, was financially secure by virtue of the vast tracts of upland endowed on the abbey which came to be used for sheep pasture. It was, however, its intimate connection with the royal families of Wales and its happy connection with the cause of Welsh independence that brought it to be identified so closely and importantly with the Welsh state.

Strata Florida was the first daughter house of Whitland Abbey and was founded by Robert FitzStephen in 1164. Robert was then Lord of that part of north Dyfed but by no means a purely Norman figure. His mother was the famous Nest, daughter of Rhys ap Tewdwr: his nephew was Gerald of Wales. The site chosen for the abbey, two miles south west of the ruins we see today, was quickly seen to be unsatisfactory. In the year following the original foundation the Lord Rhys took power over the greater part of South Wales and immediately asserted himself as patron of the new Cistercian foundation in Ystrad Fflur (Welsh for Strata Florida). Generous endowments were made and, by 1184, a new abbey was being built in the next valley to the north.

There is nothing to suggest that the pureheartedness of the monks of Strata Florida is what appealed to the Welsh. Gerald of Wales found them mean and avaricious. The abbot of Whitland had to investigate some most unholy behaviour in 1196. But during the 12th century the abbey's association with the Lord Rhys, very much the leader of southern Wales, assured its prosperity. The monks were involved with the famous histories of the Welsh nation - the *Annales Cambriae* and the

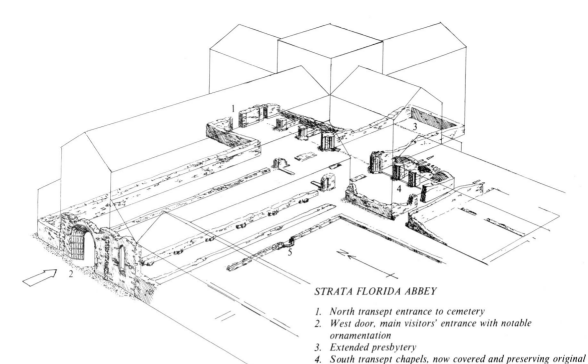

STRATA FLORIDA ABBEY

1. *North transept entrance to cemetery*
2. *West door, main visitors' entrance with notable ornamentation*
3. *Extended presbytery*
4. *South transept chapels, now covered and preserving original tiles*
5. *Site of lectern for collation reading in cloister*

Brut y Tywisogion. Members of the Lord Rhys's family were frequently laid to rest within the abbey precincts in places of high honour. With the onset of the 12th century, however, the focus of power shifted northwards to the princes of Gwynedd. The abbey did not suffer because it was, by now, thoroughly Welsh in character and centrally placed in the nation, unlike the influential abbey at Aberconway which was closely associated with Llywelyn the Great. Such was the level of political commitment at Strata Florida that in 1212 King John ordered that the abbey should be destroyed, fortunately the order was never carried out. In 1238 Llywelyn made the princes of Wales pay homage to his son David at a court held in Strata Florida.

The reign of the last Llywelyn marked desperate days for Strata Florida. At one stage the convent was close to removing from what was such a political 'hot spot'. In the final Welsh wars the abbey sustained sufficient damage to receive £78 in compensation but even greater damage was done by an ' act of God ' when, in 1285, the tower was struck by lightning and the ensuing fire wrought havoc with the buildings. In 1291 the abbey was assessed at under £100 for the purposes of taxation.

In spite of the crushing defeat of 1282, the fire of 1285 and the bitterness of the ensuing decades, Strata Florida's happiest association was, perhaps, that with the nation's greatest poet in the following century. Dafydd ap Gwilym was reputedly buried beneath a yew tree in the abbey grounds. (Visitors should not get carried away here, Leland recorded 39 'great hue trees ' within the precinct shortly after the Dissolution. The remaining yew tree may not be what they think!)

Further bad times were ahead and in the Glyndwr rebellion Strata Florida had to play host to a royal garrison. Some years later came the wretched episode when the convent and laymen of Aberconway assailed and seriously damaged the abbey of Strata Florida. Aberconway's abbot, John ap Rhys, carried on this feud with Strata Florida for some years, first from Aberconway itself and then from Cymer Abbey. The dispute may have had less to do with John's personal envy of the prestigious abbey of Strata Florida than with disputes among the patrons.

The whole episode must have crippled the abbey's finances, destroyed morale and reflected badly on the standing of this once great house. By the time of the Dissolution in 1539 the frater and infirmary were ruined and only eight monks were in the convent. The abbey's income had previously been assessed at just £118. At its height it had held over 6000 acres of land and well over 1000 sheep. It changed the face of mid Wales for the future and yet stored the nation's past in its library.

The buildings
Strata Florida was sited in one of the most beautiful and remote areas of mid Wales on level land where two deep valleys open out from the Elennith Mountains, that great mass of high moorland that dominates hundreds of square miles of the area.

Leland's description is telling - he describes the church shortly after the Dissolution as:

> larg, side ilid and crosse ilid. By is a large cloyster, the fratry and infirmitori be now mere ruines. The coemiteri wherein the cunteri about doth buri is veri large, and meanely waullid with stone. In it be 39 great hue trees. The base court or camp afore the abbay is very fair and large. The foundation of the body of the chirch was made to have been 60 foote lengyer then it is now.

The church dates from the original building - late 12th century. Unlike some other Cistercian buildings the resources of the abbey did not stretch to a substantial rebuilding after the Welsh wars, only a modest eastward extension of the presbytery. Strata Florida is, therefore, a good example of early Cistercian church planning. The aisles were separated from the nave by substantial walls the bases of which survive. Each of the two transepts contained three small chapels. Beyond the south transept ran the normal east range with sacristy and a chapter house dating from the 13th century but remodelled in the 14th century. Other arrangements, as far as they are known, were also conventional. The infirmatory mentioned by Leland probably lay to the south east.

Strata Florida is now in the hands of Cadw and many interesting artifacts from the monastery can be seen in the small museum at the entrance. The abbey is very substantially ruined, the chief pleasure it offers lies in the particular atmosphere of peace and remoteness that pervades the site. There are, however, some points of outstanding interest. The west door, of which all the masonry survives, is a rare and important expression of the Celtic spirit in Wales in the medium of architectural art. It reveals a deft adaptation of the Romanesque style and is particularly pleasing in its restraint and craftsmanship. Details in the transeptal chapels are worth noting with tiled floors surviving in the south transept. Close by is a group of gravestones. The cloister garth also holds a nice detail: the north side has a little alcove from which the collation, a reading at the close of the monastic day, was made. After the collation a glass of wine might have been enjoyed in the frater before compline, the last service of the day.

Further reading
J. Beverley Smith and W.G. Thomas, *Abaty Ystrad Fflur*. HMSO. Available at the site.
Stephen W. Williams, *The Cistercian Abbey of Strata Florida*. 1889. With details of the excavations carried out on the first, pre-1185 site.
T. Jones Pierce, Strata Florida Abbey, in *Ceredigion, the Journal of the Cardiganshire Antiquarian Society*, I, 1950.

Strata Marcella
('Pola' in some manuscripts)
Cistercian abbey

History
Strata Marcella was founded by the Prince of Powys, Owain Cyfeiliog, in 1170 and established by monks from Whitland during that period of the late 12th century which saw the expansion of the Cistercian movement in Wales. Owain was a great benefactor of the abbey, as was his son Gwenwynwyn, and Strata Marcella was patronised by his descendants throughout the 366 years of its life.

It is believed that the abbey quickly moved to a second site where it was established in 1172. At the same time the house was blemished by the indiscretions of its first abbot -

Enoch (see Llansantffraed in Elfael). According to the evidence of excavations on the site there was either a rebuilding in the early 13th century or the original building progressed very slowly. As the abbey church approached completion the convent was engaged in a serious dispute with the impoverished Cwmhir over the extent of neighbouring pastures. The monks of Strata Marcella attracted no credit to themselves in this dispute which resulted in a return to Cwmhir of land previously left to it by Gwenwynwyn. The conduct of this dispute required the services of a large number of negotiators and advisors many of whom were probably members of the convent which may have numbered 20 or 30 at the time.

Although the abbey proved itself useful to the royal house of Powys in political terms and had been rewarded with substantial benefactions the 13th century saw a decline in its fortunes. First there was the dispute with Cwmhir but the wars with England also placed the house under enormous pressure. By 1291 the assessed value for taxation was only £19, a little over half that of Cwmhir. Strata Marcella had been warmly committed to the Welsh cause and it may not have been such a bad reflection on the convent when the local magnate, John Charleton, moved to extricate the abbey from the Whitland 'family' in about 1332. He indicated that the abbey would be better for such a change and succeeded, eventually, in supplanting the convent with English monks and bringing it under the control of Buildwas Abbey. The Welsh monks were not allowed to disperse amongst their native Cistercian houses but were sent to English abbeys of the Order.

As a result of this English presence the abbey surely suffered severely in the Glyndwr rebellion. Edward Charleton confirmed the abbey's charter because, evidently, the house had suffered through fire, plunder and general destruction at the hands of Welsh insurgents. The length of the church, which had been one of the largest in Wales and one of its ecclesiastical wonders, was apparently reduced as a result. The tale of decline seems to have continued and by 1528 the convent consisted of just three monks. The abbey was, by then, substantially ruined and deteriorating rapidly. Before the Dissolution, in 1536, the abbot had already left, intent on 'cashing in' what was left of the assets. The annual income was just £64, only the lowly Grace Dieu and forlorn Cwmhir were poorer in what had once been the Welsh 'family' of Cistercian houses.

The buildings
Strata Marcella was sited on the level land of the Severn valley just to the north east of Welshpool. On the one hand the English plain beckons, on the other the Welsh hills. Our knowledge of the buildings comes from the excavations of Stephen Williams in 1890 which immediately revealed that the church was of very considerable size. The nave alone was 62 m long and 19 m wide (including the aisles). It was a cruciform church, very much comparable with Strata Florida in size and plan if one takes the view, as Williams did in 1890, that the westward 30 m of the nave were a slightly later extension. The choir and presbytery were short, again comparable to the unextended Strata Florida. Little else is known of the abbey buildings but indications of a western range, adjoining the end of the shorter nave, were uncovered together with signs of the cloister garth and the eastern range.

Nothing remains to be seen today but the site is marked close to the A483 and a commemorative stone stands at the roadside.

Further reading
Stephen W. Williams, The Cistercian Abbey of Strata Marcella. *Arch. Camb.* 1892.
J. Conway Davies, The Records of the Abbey of Ystrad Marchell. *Montgomery Collections*, Vol. 51.

Talley
Premonstratensian abbey
Church of the Blessed Virgin and John the Baptist

History
The Premonstratensian Order closely followed the Cistercians in their pursuit of a strict discipline. They were in fact canons of a reformed Augustinian order which, theoretically, made them closer to some traditional Celtic ideas of ecclesiastical organisation. Talley

was an abbey of this Order founded by the Lord Rhys in a particularly remote area of the hills above the Towy valley. The house was established probably sometime between 1184 and 1189. Rhys ap Gruffyd may have had a number of reasons for founding such a house. He had not been directly responsible for the foundation of any Welsh house and when he decided not to join the Crusades may have deemed it prudent for the safety of his soul to make such a gesture. But a more interesting motive has also been proposed which would account for his choice of this slightly obscure monastic order. Rhys was acquainted with the founders of the Premonstratensian Order in England and they may well have pointed out to him the affinities between their Order and the old Celtic traditions.

Sadly, the abbey's fortunes declined after the death of Lord Rhys. The abbot of Whitland, Peter, was in financial straits and sought to exploit the weakness of Talley by converting it into a Cistercian house. Doubtlessly Peter envisaged that the house would, in time, become little more than a grange of Whitland Abbey and thereby enhance its wealth. He managed to win over the abbot of Talley and a few of the monks but then went beyond the bounds of propriety by forcibly expelling the remaining monks with the aid of a band of armed men. The dispossessed brethren lost no time in taking their cause to Canterbury and ultimately Peter was called to order but he

managed to hold on to some of the most valuable endowments of Talley in the Teifi valley. Financially crippled, the original building plans for Talley were now curtailed and a more modest church was completed than that originally intended.

Having been founded by a Welsh prince it is hardly surprising that Talley was closely committed to the Welsh cause in the wars of the 13th century. Long before the end of the struggle the house was impoverished and in 1278 was taken into royal custody. Following this event, which was almost unheard of in Wales, it seems that the King tried to supplant the Welsh with English canons. It was alleged that the canons of Talley supported their concubines and offspring out of revenues that should have been directed to the abbey's proper programme of assisting the poor and sick. The canons were also accused of drunkenness. Although the motive behind such accusations is all too clear it was, unfortunately, not unknown for other houses in Wales to show such lapses at this time. Whatever the truth, the King seems to have got his way and Talley was put in the care of Welbeck Abbey; it had previously been directly under the care of St Jean of Amiens.

Little is known of the later life of the house. Records suggest that it continued to be afflicted by misrule and consequent impoverishment. The taxation of 1291 valued the house at £62 and the Valor Ecclesiasticus

TALLEY ABBEY

1. *Abandoned nave, broken lines show the original building intentions*
2. *The nave area as completed*
3. *Sacristy*
4. *East Range*
5. *Cloister area*

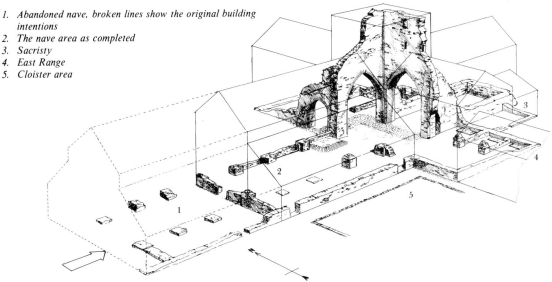

of 1535 put the annual income at £153. The house then had a convent of eight canons.

The buildings

Talley is properly known by the Welsh as Talyllychau, a reference to the lakes by which the ruins stand between steep hills half a dozen miles north of Llandeilo. Of the buildings only the church is known to us with part of the cloister. The church speaks eloquently of the troubled history of the abbey. It was originally conceived as a cruciform building with north and south aisles along the length of the nave, three chapels in each transept and a full range of conventual buildings. The crossing tower, transepts and presbytery were completed together with a little sacristy on the south side of the presbytery. The south wall of the nave and the arcades for the aisles were built to a length of 46 m. It would have been a church to rival any of the Cistercian churches but Abbot Peter of Whitland's ambition put paid to the hopes of Talley's canons and the building was severely curtailed. The north aisle was never completed, the nave was shortened to 23 m (just four bays of the arcade) but the conventual buildings were built.

Seen across the lake from the B4302 the ruins present an idyllic spectacle but sadly little remains of this interesting house. The crossing tower still stands to near its original height in two of its walls. The site of the transeptal chapels is clearly seen and the arch of the intended north aisle stands against the crossing tower. All these date from the original twelfth-century buildings. The ruins are best viewed with the intentions of the builders in mind rather than their achievements. Part of the cloister garth is exposed with the doorway leading into the south aisle. In the south transept the base of the night stairs informs us that the east range followed a typical monastic plan.

Further reading

J. Beverley Smith and B.H. St J. O'Neil, *Talley Abbey*. HMSO 1967.

Tintern
Cistercian abbey

History

The ruins of Tintern Abbey are widely renowned as some of the most extensive and picturesque in Britain. Tintern was the first Cistercian house in Wales but was never closely involved in national affairs and may be regarded as essentially English.

The region around Chepstow, known in the middle ages as 'Striguil', was the first area in Wales to fall under Norman domination. The great castle at Chepstow was established by William FitzOsbern by 1071 with a Benedictine priory springing up beside it. Sixty years later Cistercian monks from L'Aumone, in the diocese of Chartres, had already established the first house of their order in Britain at Waverley and now came to the Wye valley north of Chepstow to begin a new foundation. William FitzRichard, then Lord of Striguil, gave them a level stretch of land in the dramatic valley some half dozen miles north of the castle. The first convent settled there in 1131.

The first abbey was a smaller affair than the one we see now but on much the same scale as the Benedictine priories already established at Brecon, Ewenny and Chepstow itself. Although Tintern established daughter houses at Kingswood, just across the Severn in Gloucestershire, and later in southern Ireland it could not be said that it extended the Cistercian influence in Wales itself. It was evidently well endowed and, being outside the main arena of political and military activity surrounding the Welsh struggle for independence, it was financially secure. So, early in the 13th century, the convent was able to begin a complete and impressive rebuilding of the monastery. In spite of some losses in a conflict in 1233 the building programme continued and, by 1270, the magnificent church was begun. By the end of the 13th century, before the building programme was complete, the abbey was valued at £108 with more than 3000 sheep and 3000 acres of land. This was the height of its power and wealth, a period when nearly every other house in Wales was going through extreme difficulties. It was not, however, a period marked by great moral endeavour. There were petty squabbles regarding the maintenance of weirs on the River Wye and the abbey

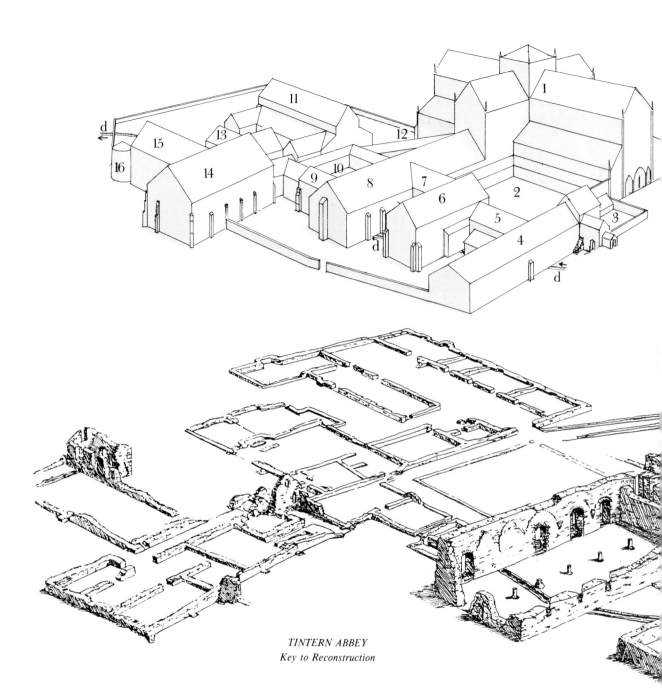

TINTERN ABBEY
Key to Reconstruction

1. The Church	*9.* Reredorter
2. Main Cloister	*10.* Infirmary Cloister
3. Lay Brothers' Cloister and entrance to Church	*11.* Infirmary
4. Lay Brothers' quarters	*12.* Alley leading directly to the Church from Infirmary
5. Kitchen	*13.* Infirmary Kitchen
6. Frater	*14.* Abbot's Hall
7. Warming House	*15.* Abbot's Lodging
8. West Range, monks' dormitory above, novices' lodgings below	*16.* Dovecote
	d. Drain running beneath Kitchen and Reredorter

appears to have been responsible for a serious interruption of navigation on the river. Officials, sent to put matters right by lowering the weirs, were assaulted by the monks. Walter Map also records the punitive attitude of the monks towards a man who stole apples from their orchard: he was summarily hanged. At about this time one of the monks managed to insinuate himself into the priorship of Goldcliff (q.v.) by dint of a forged papal note and much to the detriment of that Benedictine house.

Although not directly afflicted by the ravages of the Glyndwr rebellion Tintern found itself in straitened circumstances in the years following. Like the other houses in the area, particularly Monmouth, it could derive little from its holdings and failed to collect taxes on the crown's behalf because of the devastation in the aftermath of the rebellion. A full convent was maintained, however, and at the Dissolution in 1539 there were 13 monks. The abbey's income had been valued at £192 in 1535 making it one of the richest possessions to come into the Crown's hands out of Wales.

The buildings

Tintern is rightly famed for the beauty of its setting and the splendour of its ruins. Wordsworth described the

> . . . steep and lofty cliffs,
> Which on a wild secluded scene impress
> Thoughts of more deep seclusion . . .

It says much for the beauty of the ruins that they can be seen to enhance one of the most beautiful valleys in the country.

The ruins are principally those of the re-built church of the late 13th century but the original building was quite a bit smaller. It was a simple cruciform church which was similar in size (51 m long) and plan to the earliest Cistercian buildings in Britain at Waverley. The conventual ranges were of normal plan around a small cloister with a frater running along the length of the range furthest from the church. In Tintern this meant the north range because the builders chose to erect the church a little distance from the river which constricted the possible site for the conventual buildings. These were all placed on the north side of the church.

The east range was extended and developed during the later part of the 12th century and a reredorter was added.

The first substantial alterations, however, were not made to the church but to the frater and western ranges. The new frater was larger and followed the later fashion of being built at right angles to the cloister, a kitchen and a warming house were placed on either side. New lodgings were built for the abbot and for the lay brothers at the same time. The major rebuilding of the church began in 1270 and involved the gradual and total destruction of the old church to make way for the large and quite magnificent building that was to replace it. Together with the addition of a large infirmary this established the layout of the monastery for the rest of its life. Later additions in the 14th and 15th centuries included a further provision for the abbot and a restructuring of the infirmary and its kitchens. A little cloister filled the space between the infirmary and the monks' dormitory. An alley led straight to the church from the south-east corner of this cloister.

The new church was the grandest monastic building ever built in Wales with stone vaulted ceilings of a height that was exceptional in the country. It was a cruciform building with side aisles extending along the length of both nave and presbytery. The monks' choir and presbytery took up well over half of the length of the church suggesting the reduced role of the lay brethren in the latter half of the abbey's life.

On such a large site it is worth drawing the visitor's attention to a few points. The site is in the hands of Cadw which maintains an excellent exhibition at the entrance. This should be perused before inspecting the site itself. The church is so dominant among the ruins that little need be said about it. Although mostly unroofed it is otherwise a ruin in excellent condition if that is not a contradiction in terms. The magnificent west front with delicate tracery on the doorway and windows is of particular note. Within the church and also in the doorway to the cloister there is much fine masonry to be observed. The junction of the roof of the east range to the north transept can be seen from the string on the church wall. This gives a fair idea of the height of the range. The range consisted of a book room and vestry (fine doorway), chapter house (ruined but for the bases of the pillars supporting the vaulted ceiling) and the monks' dormitory over the novices' lodgings (substantial remains). Some of the most complete remains are of the warming house and part of the frater which preserves the stairway leading to a pulpit from which a reading was made during meal times. The western range contains good remains of the cellarer's buildings particularly around the 'outer parlour' and its porch. The provision for the lay brethren is easily seen in this range with their special access to both cloister and church. Other parts of the site are mostly ruined to the foundations.

Further reading

Although the serious student would need to study the work of Brakspear (1934) the new and quite beautiful little guide produced by Cadw should not be missed. This gives great attention to the visual aspects of the site and its treatment by various artists is well illustrated. The original HMSO guide by O.E. Craster gives a concise treatment of the history.

Usk
Benedictine priory of nuns

History

Usk Priory was the only non-Cistercian house of nuns in Wales. The date of the foundation is not known but the nuns believed that Richard de Clare, known as 'Strongbow', was the founder. If the tradition is correct then the priory was probably founded sometime before 1135 and dates from the period of the building of the castle and town of Usk. Between 1130 and 1160 there were about 50 Benedictine houses for nuns built and Usk would have been founded right at the beginning of that period of expansion. The nuns seem to have used a church already in existence to which was added a north aisle so that the convent could have free use of the original church.

There are some records of monks serving the church, particularly in 1330, but who the monks were is not clear. It has been assumed (Knowles and Hadcock) that the convent was for a full complement of 13 nuns but again no record confirms this. The priory was dis-

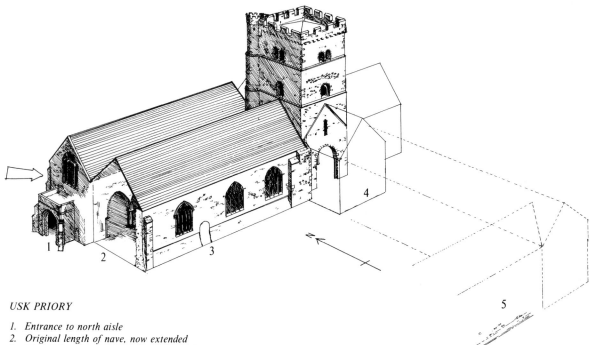

USK PRIORY

1. *Entrance to north aisle*
2. *Original length of nave, now extended*
3. *Site of door leading into church from cloister*
4. *Clear signs of transepts and presbytery*
5. *Private building has slight remains of the south range*

solved in 1536 after its annual income had been assessed at £55. Six nuns were present at the Dissolution.

The buildings

In essence the priory church was a simple cruciform church of modest size and without aisles. This original church, with a sturdy crossing tower, was 37 m long. It would appear that in the 12th century the nave was extended by about 3 m and a north aisle added to give greater space for the parochial use of the church. Also dating from the period of the nuns' use of the church was the addition of two porches giving entrance to the north aisle in the 15th century. The conventual buildings attached to the south side of the church in the normal manner with a cloister abutting the south nave wall.

Of the nuns' church there are considerable remains as the building, like many other Bene-

dictine churches, continues in use today. Unfortunately the transepts and presbytery are lost to us, the space under the tower being now used as the chancel. The indications of the lost parts can be clearly seen on the outside of the tower. The most telling remnant of the conventual use of the church is in the fine transitional Norman arcade which was built so that the church could be extended to accommodate both nuns and parishioners. The two porches and windows in the north aisle have pleasant details but it should be noted that the modern nave has been further extended in more recent years, the original nave ended on the same line as the north aisles. In the early period of the priory, before the first extension, the nave probably presented an elaborate west front and entrance.

Of the conventual buildings the chief remnant is the attractive gatehouse to the west of the church. The Gothic mansion south of the church does, however, appear to retain some stonework from the south range of the

The gatehouse of Usk Priory.

priory, parts of which stood to first floor level in the last century. There is no public access to this part of the priory.

Further reading

S.W. Williams, Architectural Notes upon Usk Church. *Arch. Camb.* 1886.

Valle Crucis
Cistercian abbey

History

With the exception of Grace Dieu which was an English foundation, Valle Crucis was the last Cistercian house to be established in Wales. Today its ruins are among the most complete and beautiful in the Principality.

It was founded in 1201 by Madoc ap Gruffydd Maelor who was the ruler of Powys, faithful ally of Llewelyn the Great. The 'mother' church was Strata Marcella, the only other Cistercian house in Powys. Although the house was established with a full convent it was never large. The evidence of the buildings themselves reveals much of the history of Valle Crucis. For example, it is apparent that a large and probably accidental fire blighted the very first buildings erected but that otherwise it did not receive much, if any, damage during the Welsh wars. The documentary evidence for this lies in the tiny sum of £4 paid by Edward I as compensation for war damage in 1284. On the other hand it must be noted that Edward had been quite niggardly in this respect towards certain abbeys that had made common with the Welsh cause. Valle Crucis had certainly allied itself with its mother house, Strata Marcella, during the 13th century and would not have expected generosity after the Welsh defeat. The figure of £14 at which the abbey was valued for the taxation of 1291 suggests that it was very far from being wealthy.

Building repairs to the western half of the church in the early 15th century suggest that Valle Crucis may have suffered some damage during the Glyndwr rebellion but otherwise the

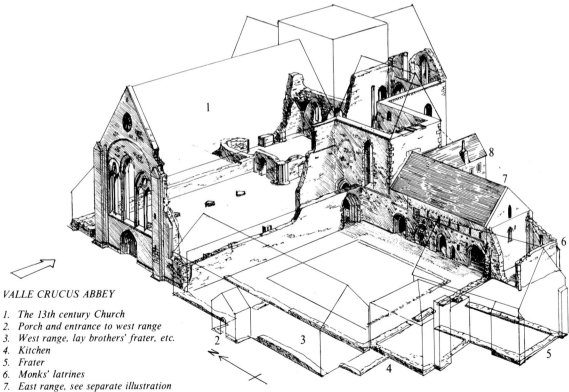

VALLE CRUCUS ABBEY

1. *The 13th century Church*
2. *Porch and entrance to west range*
3. *West range, lay brothers' frater, etc.*
4. *Kitchen*
5. *Frater*
6. *Monks' latrines*
7. *East range, see separate illustration*
8. *Abbot's lodgings*

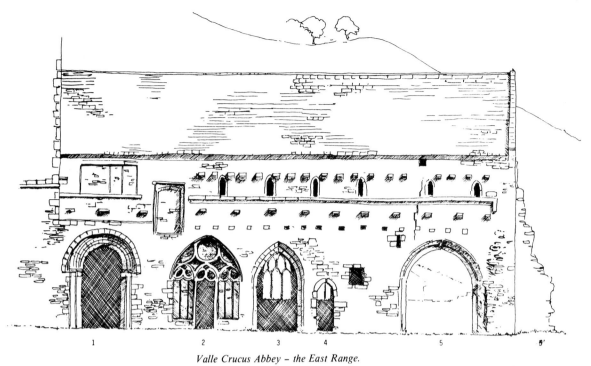

Valle Crucis Abbey – the East Range.

1. Entrance to Sacristy.   2. Book Cupboard.   3. Entrance to Chapter House.   4. Day Stairs up to Dormitory.   5. Passage.

abbey appears to have led a quiet life and, compared with other Welsh Cistercian houses, a prosperous one. In its last years, however, the house was scandalised by its state of moral and physical decline. The abbot, Roger Salusbury, was a notorious highwayman whose 'gang' operated around the Oxford area. Before it was dissolved in 1538 the annual income was assessed at £188 making it second only to Tintern in wealth. At the Dissolution there were six monks in the convent.

The buildings

Being a late foundation the church at Valle Crucis was more of a piece than many other abbeys of the period since no substantial rebuilding took place and the whole building makes a consistent expression of thirteenth-century architectural ideas. Coupled with the typically wild situation of the abbey in a narrow valley amongst steep hills, Valle Crucis makes a most attractive site, ruined though it is. The thirteenth-century building programme was, however, seriously interrupted by fire so that some parts bear evidence of

being built later in that century. The church was not large, being only 56 m long from the presbytery to the west end, and not as long as some Cistercian naves in Wales. It was cruciform in plan, each transept having two small chapels. The nave of five bays had aisles on both sides but the presbytery was without aisles. The conventual buildings were laid out at the same time as the church in the normal arrangement of west, east and south ranges. The frater in the south range was built on a north-south axis in the later fashion.

In the 14th century the east range was rebuilt with a fine, square, vaulted chapter house and the monks' dormitory was taken over to accommodate the abbot's lodgings towards the end of the abbey's life. Minor additions were also made to the western range and kitchen in the 14th century when a small gatehouse was also erected on the cellarer's wing.

The remains are in the hands of Cadw and are of exceptional interest to anyone interested in monastic architecture. Apart from the considerable remains of the thirteenth-century church the eastern range survives almost intact. In the church the west and east front are of special interest. The west for the beauty of its exterior wall, the east for the originality of design of its exterior. In the east range the chapter house is as complete an example as will be found anywhere in these islands in a Cistercian monastery. The vaulted roof, book cupboard in the north wall and repaired west light are features of particular interest. Close to the chapter h e entrance a narrow stairway leads up to the monks' dormitory which was later adapted for the abbot's lodgings. In the cloister are indications of the sheltered walkway - holes for the roof timbers and corbels for the roof run along the wall of the east range and the south transept. The transept indicates that the roof of the cloister walk was originally higher.

Further reading

Cadw has produced one of its attractive new handbooks to the site written chiefly by D. H. Evans. This contains a comprehensive description of the site and its history. The original HMSO Blue guide was written by C. A. Ralegh Radford and is, therefore, also to be recommended.

Whitland
Cistercian abbey

History

The great Cistercian abbey of Clairvaux in France established two houses in Wales, Whitland (1140) and Margam (1147). Margam was always within the Anglo-Norman sphere of influence but Whitland, although initially outside the area of native control, soon fell into Welsh hands and became one of their most important houses.

The original foundation is imprecisely recorded. A colony of monks was invited to settle in South Wales by Bishop Bernard of St David's. The first home for this colony was at Trefgarn but there is still debate as to whether this was the Trefgarn north of Haverfordwest or a site much closer to Whitland itself, near Lampeter Velfrey. Whatever the truth the monks had settled at the final site north of the town of Whitland,

described by Leland as 'in a vast wood', by about 1151. This site was the gift of one John of Torrington. The foundation was an immediate success and is reputed to have supported 100 monks. With the rise to power of the Lord Rhys, Whitland developed as a Welsh house and was patronised by Rhys himself. The abbey remained, throughout its history, one of the most passionately nationalistic Welsh houses. This was especially significant in view of the fact that it was also the 'mother house' of the Welsh Cistercians.

The little that is known of the history of Whitland chiefly reflects the volatile times through which it lived. When, in 1188, Archbishop Baldwin of Canterbury preached for the Crusade at Whitland, 12 archers from St Clears who had committed murder 'signed on'. At the end of the 12th century the abbey went through a crisis under the abbacy of Peter, described by Gerald of Wales in the most scathing terms. Although Gerald was often in conflict with the Cistercians who may have thwarted some of his ambitions, there seems some justification for the accusation that Peter had brought the house of Whitland to a state of ruination. Peter's conduct in the affair with Talley Abbey (q.v.) presented posterity with the impression of an ambitious and machinating man. Therefore, when Gerald suggests that the Welsh abbot Cadwgan (1203-1215) had manipulated his way into the abbacy of Whitland it would be unwise to put the story down simply to Gerald's sense of aggrievement.

In the 13th century Whitland paid dearly for its espousal of the Welsh cause. In 1257, when the last Llywelyn was asserting himself in North Wales, a Norman force broke down the gate of the abbey, set about the monks and robbed the lay brothers. In the cemetery, servants were killed and the marauders made off with substantial possessions from the abbey. At the end of the wars Whitland, a breeding ground of resistance, received no compensation for damages. Thus in 1291, when the abbey was valued for taxation, it appeared to be thoroughly impoverished. In spite of its importance as the founding house of Strata Florida, Strata Marcella and Cwmhir (and thus indirectly of another four houses), its possession of 1100 sheep and over 5000 acres, it was valued at only £43. The abbey appears to have suffered from continuous mismanage-

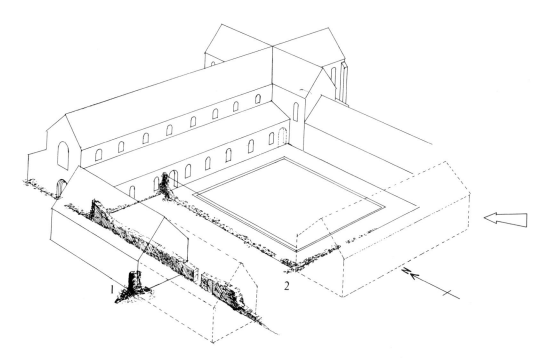

ment and by 1330 was, if anything, in a worse plight. When the Glyndwr rebellion flared up at the beginning of the 15th century Whitland was, naturally, much involved on the Welsh side of the conflict. Though the abbot was penalised for this the sympathies of the house were not altered and by 1440 Whitland was in a pitiful state. The buildings were apparently damaged and burnt and the revenues enormously reduced. Poorly governed, the convent consisted of just eight monks together with their servants. The Welsh abbots were often criticised for their lax and ineffective management: in 1491 Maurice ap Ieuan was deposed from Whitland and took his management techniques to Strata Marcella which suffered as a result.

A final, unsavoury event is recorded in 1496 when a monk from Neath, staying at Whitland Abbey, killed a priest in the cloister. In spite of this catalogue of ills it is apparent that Whitland still continued to function as the senior house of the Welsh Cistercian family. The majority of the Cistercian houses of Wales could trace their origins back to Whitland and therefore afforded special respect

WHITLAND ABBEY
A surviving fragment of the conventional buildings, possibly belonging to the cellarer's range or even part of an entrance building.

to that abbey.

In 1535 the annual income of Whitland was assessed prior to the Dissolution at £135. There was still a convent of eight monks but when the house was dissolved in 1539 only five were present.

The buildings

Whitland, like several other Cistercian houses, was sited on a broad valley floor just where it emerges from the high hills of the Welsh uplands. It was a position that gave the abbey close access to hill pastures for its flocks of sheep and also to the arable lands and watermills of the Taff valley. The church erected on the final site was typical of that early phase of Cistercian building in the 12th century. It was a cruciform building with aisles either side of the 47 m long nave. Each transept had two chapels whilst a short presbytery extended east of the crossing over which there does not appear to have been a tower. It seems that the abbey was never able to elaborate on or extend the original plan to any significant degree, doubtless a reflection of its continual poverty.

Our knowledge of the buildings is largely dependent on the excavations carried out by Collier in 1926 which revealed indications of the normal plan of conventual buildings. The plan of the cloister, however, presents some problems with its unusually wide 'lane' between the cloister garth and the cellarer's buildings (west range). The relative length of the lay brothers' choir and the existence of this lane may be evidence of a large number of lay brethren in the early days of the abbey. The lane was designed to separate the busy, worldly life of the cellarer from the religious life of the cloister: it may have extended right through the south range.

The remains, such as they are, stand on private ground but can be adequately viewed from the tracks and lanes that partially enclose the site about one mile north of Whitland. This site is more atmospheric than informative but a little of the church outline can be discerned opposite the farmyard where the line of the presbytery can be seen abutting the Llanboidy road. Close perusal will indicate the position of the transepts and the wall to the west of this occupies the line of the nave's south wall.

The east wall of the west range would appear to be standing but has clearly been rebuilt a number of times. One genuine relic of the conventual buildings unfortunately defies interpretation. The broken, ivy clad fragment that extends west from the site of the west range may have been part of a gatehouse, a guesthouse or even a reredorter. The whole site, in view of its considerable importance in Welsh history, deserves better preservation and presentation.

Priory cells
Priory cells of the Benedictine Order

Bassaleg
Near Newport, Gwent. Founded 1116 by Robert of Hay, granted to Glastonbury. 'Farmed' c.1235. Monks presumably withdrawn at this time.

Cardiff
Founded between 1102 and 1107 by Robert FitzHamon. Granted to Tewkesbury Abbey. The cell ceased to exist in the early 14th century. The church itself was steadily eroded by the River Taff leaving no remains since the 18th century.

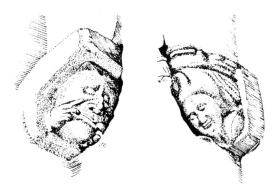

Carvings in the chancel of
Cardigan Priory Church.

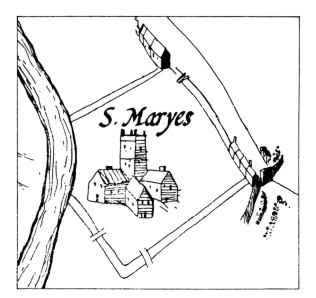

ST MARY'S CARDIFF
As depicted on a map of 1610.

Cardigan
Founded c.1100 probably by Gilbert de Clare. Originally belonging to Gloucester Abbey, Rhys ap Gruffydd expelled the English monks and granted the priory to Chertsey Abbey. The monastic portion of the church survives as the present chancel of the town church with some fine details - the monks' door in the south-east corner and two carved heads against the chancel arch.
See E.M. Pritchard, *Cardigan Priory in the Olden Days*, 1904.

Kidwelly
Founded 1106-1115. Belonged to Sherborne Abbey. Dissolved 1539. Fine, cruciform church survives with exceptionally wide chancel arch reminiscent of Cardigan. Conventual buildings were to the north. The site is impressively dominated by the castle across the river - a reminder of the Norman domination through religion and force.
See D.D. Jones, *The History of Kidwelly*, Carmarthen 1908.

Llanbadarn Fawr
A Celtic monastery of great renown. In its declining years it was granted to the Benedictines of Gloucester (1116) who were soon ejected (1136). The monastery then continued its former life which appears to have ceased by the mid 13th century.
See E.G. Bowen, *A History of Llanbadarn Fawr*, Llanbadarn Fawr 1979.

Llandovery
Founded c.1110 by Richard FitzPons. Notorious on account of Gerald of Wales' reference to the licentious behaviour of the monks as a result of which the house was dissolved by Rhys ap Gruffydd.

Llangennith
At the west end of the Gower peninsula, founded c.1110 by Richard Earl of Warwick. Continuing association with the monastic cell on the nearby island of Burry Holms. An alien priory, it survived until the mid 15th century. The church remains intact and the monks' entrance in the south wall can be seen from

inside. On Burry Holms are interesting remains of the tiny monastery excavated 1965-7.

See F.G. Cowley, The Priory at Llangennith in *Glamorgan Historian*, Vol. 5.

Also D.B. Hague, The Burry Holms Excavations 1965-6, in the *Journal of the Gower Society*, Vol. 17.

Llangua

Near Abergavenny, founded probably *c.*1110. An alien cell belonging to the Abbey of Lire

Kidwelly Priory.

in France. Dissolved and granted to the Carthusian house of Sheen in Surrey *c.*1420. No remains but the local church was presumably associated with the cell.

Priory cells

Priory cells of the Cluniac Order

Malpas

Near Newport, Gwent. Founded before 1122 by Winibald of Caerleon. Mother house was Montacute in Somerset. Suppressed 1539. No remains but the interesting church, destroyed in 1849, is the subject of a number of antiquarian illustrations.

St Clear's

Founded between 1147 and 1184. Under the Abbey of St Martin des Champs in Paris. In 1279 the monks were reckoned to be dissolute. It was dissolved in 1414. No remains of the conventual buildings to the south but the church retains the splendid chancel arch of the monastic period.

Lesser houses of the Augustinian Order

St Kynemark

Near Chepstow. Very little is known of the monastery which was probably founded in the 13th century or adapted at that time from an older Celtic institution. It was suppressed in 1535. Excavations between 1962 and 1965 revealed two parallel ranges of conventual buildings (dated *c.*1250) but no church.

See G.A.S. Butler, St Kynemark's Priory, Chepstow in *Monmouthshire*, Vol. 2.

St Tudwal's

On St Tudwal's East Island, off the Gwynedd coast near Abersoch. Possibly a Celtic religious site and, by the 13th century, a house of the Order of St Augustine. Little is known of the priory's history. It was dissolved in 1535. The scant remains have been excavated to reveal a tiny complex of church, sacristy, workshop and other buildings.

See D.B. Hague, The Medieval Church on the Island of St Tudwal, *Caernarvonshire Historical Society Transactions*, 1960. RCAHM Caernarvonshire West.

Glossary

Where appropriate the terminology of monastic life and buildings has been simplified, I have tried to avoid aumbries and dorters when cupboards and dormitories are more comprehensible. Explanation of some terms is, however, necessary.

Abbey	Senior house of an Order, presided over by an abbot.
Aisles	Passages either side of the nave or presbytery.
Arcade	Line of arches usually separating the nave or presbytery from the aisles whilst supporting the main wall of the church.
Cellarer	The monk in charge of the general stores of the convent. His store rooms normally occupied the west wing.
Chapter house	Principal office in the secular buildings where the life of the convent was ordered.
Choir	Central part of the monks' church where the services were sung.
Cloister	Enclosed but unroofed area adjoining the church where the monks would relax, read and study.
Compline	The last service of the day.
Convent	Collective title for the community of monks, nuns or canons.
Day stairs	Stairway used by the convent passing from the dormitory to the church during daytime.
Dormitory	Technically the 'dorter', where the convent slept. This long room was divided by screens to give the monks some degree of privacy.
Frater	The dining hall or refectory.
Gatehouse	Principal entrance to the monastic precinct.
Grange	Farm belonging to an abbey.
Infirmary	Monastic hospital.
Lane	Passage separating the west range from the cloister.
Nave	Part of the church west of the crossing.
Night stairs	Stairs leading from the monks' dormitory to the church when attending matins (2 a.m.).
Novice	A monk under training to become a full member of the convent.
Precinct	The total area occupied by the abbey buildings and its immediate surrounds.
Presbytery	Eastern part of the monks' church containing the high altar.
Priory	Monastery subject to an abbey and governed by a prior.
Pulpitum	Stone screen separating the monks' church from the western part of the church.
Reredorter	Next to the dormitory, the monks' latrine block, built over the main drain.
Sacristy	Small room adjoining the church where consecrated vessels, often very valuable, were kept. The office of the sacrist who was in charge of such items.
Sedilia	Seat in the presbytery where clergy officiating in ceremonies would sit.
Slype	Passage leading from the cloister through the east range. Often the monks' rule of silence would be relaxed here.
Transepts	Transepts formed the two short arms of a cruciform (cross shaped) church.
Warming room	A room where a fire was kept burning, particularly in winter, for the comfort of the convent.